## DATE DUE

| | | | |
|---|---|---|---|
| AP16 01 | | | |
| AP03 01 | | | |
| | | | |
| | | | |
| | | | |
| | | | |
| | | | |
| | | | |
| | | | |
| | | | |
| | | | |
| | | | |
| | | | |
| | | | |
| | | | |
| | | | |
| | | | |
| | | | |
| | | | |
| | | | |
| | | | |

Demco, Inc. 38-293

The
Fear
of
Crime

# The
# Fear
# of
# Crime

Richard Harris

INTRODUCTION BY
NICHOLAS DeB. KATZENBACH

FREDERICK A. PRAEGER, *Publishers*
New York • Washington • London

FREDERICK A. PRAEGER, *Publishers*
111 Fourth Avenue, New York, N.Y. 10003 U.S.A.
5, Cromwell Place, London S.W. 7, England

Published in the United States of America in 1969
by Frederick A. Praeger, Inc., Publishers

Library of Congress Catalog Card Number: 74–92865

Except for the Introduction, the contents of this book
originally appeared, under the title "The Turning Point,"
in *The New Yorker.*

Printed in the United States of America

For
William Shawn

# CONTENTS

# INTRODUCTION

*By Nicholas deB. Katzenbach*

T H E fear of crime is a reality in the United States today. So is crime, dramatized quarterly by F.B.I. statistics. The failure of our political institutions to respond sensibly to either the fear or the reality is skillfully described and documented in Mr. Harris's account of the enactment of the Omnibus Crime Bill during 1967–68.

One could view this book as simply a vignette of recent Congressional history—with a surfeit of villains and a discouraging shortage of heroes. It would be worth reading if only for its insights into the legislative process— a process little examined and less understood. But the problem it highlights in this legislative setting is more serious. That it is still with us—and, without public understanding, can rend the fabric of our political institutions— ought to be obvious to any observer of recent municipal elections. The issues that were debated and discussed and unsatisfactorily resolved in the Omnibus Crime Bill are still the issues debated and discussed—with all the same

1

demagogic appeals and irrelevant rhetoric—in Los Angeles, Detroit, New York, and elsewhere.

There is little one can add to the specifics of THE FEAR OF CRIME. The Congressional process is well described. But perhaps an introduction can remind the reader of some of the background that makes the subject so important, the debate so seemingly fruitless, and the politics of elected officials—struggling between conscience and an electorate—so difficult.

There are many ingredients to the confusing calls for "law and order," and, while these do not have to be mixed up together, they have become so. In this respect, liberals and conservatives, intellectuals and rednecks, racists and civil libertarians, adults and juveniles are all contributors to confusion. The Omnibus Crime Bill itself documents, through its "omnibus" character—and through the underlying biases of the debate—the confusion of the country as a whole.

Knowing how we got here is important for understanding where we are—and how the Congress of the United States could overwhelmingly approve such a bad law.

That story began in the South, and the principal actors were Martin Luther King, Jr., and Robert F. Kennedy. It was the story of sit-ins, freedom buses, freedom marches —of Montgomery, Ole Miss, Selma on the one hand, and attempted governmental repression by state authorities (Governors Barnett, Patterson, and Wallace, and Sheriff Clark), on the other. The moral issues then seemed clear enough, and most of white America outside the South supported Mr. Kennedy and Dr. King. Officially sanctioned segregation was clearly doomed. The essential active political support of civil-rights groups, the organized bar, organized labor, church and women's groups was forthcoming and resulted in the Civil Rights Act of 1964 and the Voting Rights Act of 1965.

But, unfortunately, the issues that seemed on the surface so clear could be and were very differently viewed by different actors. Dr. King, for example, constantly preached nonviolent disobedience of "unjust" laws. Attorney General Kennedy shared Dr. King's racial objectives but, as the nation's chief law-enforcement officer and as a knowledgeable student and practitioner of democratic politics, placed his reliance on the Constitution, the federal courts, and, eventually, Congress. He was anxious to get demonstrations off the streets and into the courts. This was possible because Dr. King's "unjust" laws were almost always also un-Constitutional; the federal courts, especially the courageous Fifth Circuit Court of Appeals, enjoined their use against Negroes, and—with considerable effort, including a reluctant use of the armed forces— the Justice Department could secure the enforcement of their decisions. Thus, in a curious way, Dr. King, who preached disobedience to law, could be allied with the Justice Department and the federal courts in law enforcement, and Southern governors, school boards, and sheriffs, who pleaded for "law and order," could be fairly cast in the roll of law-violators. As a result, it was possible for our political processes to respond effectively—although in a cumbersome and slow fashion—to an essential resolution of one important aspect of the racial problem.

I do not suggest that this was satisfactory to all involved, or even generally understood. Whether or not he accepted the distinction between "unjust" and "un-Constitutional," Dr. King did, in fact, obey court orders and confine his demonstration techniques to direct violation of un-Constitutional laws or Constitutionally protected demonstrations. RFK chafed under the slowness of the judicial process but saw it as the only alternative to violence and a breakdown of our political system. Southern politicians bitterly resented the alliance of a brash young Attorney General, Dr. King, and the Supreme Court in breaking down what was essentially a caste system. Southern law-enforcement officials not only saw their concepts of law enforcement destroyed but—in many cases honestly —also doubted their capacity to maintain any kind of law and order in a context that reversed the past by requiring them to protect Negroes from whites. Liberal white politicians were often bitter in their criticisms of the Attorney General for not sending more U.S. marshals or more U.S. troops. Whatever their view of *due process of law* in other contexts, they had little patience with the effort to apply it evenhandedly to Southern segregationists.

More interesting, perhaps, was the impact of these dramatic events in the South on some very dedicated young college and high school students outside the South. A large number of young people participated in demonstrations and worked summers to help in the civil-rights movement. That this could be dangerous was both obvious and savored. There was constant harassment and intimidation by local sheriffs. State officials were to be distrusted. Police were dishonest. The federal government procrastinated. Three young civil-rights workers were murdered in cold blood by members of the KKK in Mississippi with the connivance of local law-enforcement officers. (To me it was of the utmost importance that this brutal act should not and did not go unpunished. But I suspect this near miracle of law enforcement—which took over three years to accomplish—went almost unnoticed among the young.)

Out of this experience in the South from 1961 to 1964, one could draw many variant conclusions. On the one hand was the relative success of federal political response; the March on Washington (which really almost became Establishment by virtue of the breadth of its support); the 1964 Civil Rights Act; and, most important, the refusal of the white South itself to sanction a violent response to major—from its viewpoint—change. On the other hand, one could point to the effectiveness of direct political action (forgetting any constitutional points), to the slowness and compromising response of political institutions, to the brutality and heavyhandedness of police acts.

Out of this period it was possible to learn that law and

justice could equate—roughly, and with much sweat and pain. It was also possible to learn—indeed, I learned it, too—that government could be cynical and corrupt, that law could in these United States be an instrument of wrong, and that it was terribly difficult to put that kind of a system right.

"Law and order" was the constant promise of Southern governors and sheriffs. It was—ironically—also the appeal of the federal government. The particular "law and order" was not the same. Perhaps this fact increased the cynicism of the young. Yet, I suspect that the political support for civil rights that the Kennedy and Johnson administrations were able to muster was in large part due to the Constitutional arguments and to the blatant disrespect for law that Southern officials exhibited. There is much latent racism in our society, but there is also much respect for the symbols of government.

Let me shift to another subject—crime. It *was* another subject in 1961, because no one then thought of Dr. King's sit-ins as "crimes" in the ordinary sense of the word, and, of course, they were not. They were committed for political purposes; they were not even technically "crimes," because the statutes they violated were themselves un-Constitutional. But, in the eyes of the civil-rights movement and many young people, they continued to be political acts, and vindication was a political victory, not a legal one—measured not by Constitutional doctrine but by political results.

For the past several years, crime in the traditional sense —murder, mugging, robbery, theft—has been increasing at an accelerating rate, especially in major cities. Although Attorney General Kennedy launched a major campaign against organized crime, relatively little has been done to deal with street crimes, which are, and should be, the responsibility of local law-enforcement officials. The sheer increase in volume of these crimes has been enough to warrant national public concern. But the problem took on political overtones as a result of the attention given to "law and order," to civil-rights activities, ghetto riots, radical student demonstrations, and the growing number of anti-Vietnam acts of protest. In addition, a series of Supreme Court decisions extended Constitutional protections to accused criminals in ways that undoubtedly have made life a great deal more difficult for already harassed, undermanned, and underpaid police forces. The Court also decided a number of cases with respect to censorship that have resulted in freer availability of written and visual material highly offensive to most Americans.

There is no real connection between the rise in street crime and other forms of civil disorder. If there had been no "Negro revolution," no civil-rights movement, no riots, no war in Vietnam, no political furor about four-letter words, and no change in the law or its interpretation by the Supreme Court, we would still have a serious and growing crime problem. We would still have a fear of crime. But it might be possible to discuss the problem rationally and attack it sensibly as President Johnson's Crime Commission sought to do.

We have had a lot of "crime" as a result of essentially political acts—"crime" committed by people whose motivation was not personal gain and who in no ordinary sense were criminals, even though they violated laws that were both "just" and Constitutional; one may feel that the Vietnamese war or the draft is "unjust," but there is no injustice in a law that makes criminal "sitting in" selective service offices or punishes those who destroy selective service records. These are difficult problems for law-enforcement officials and the courts to handle, precisely because they do not fit the concept of our criminal justice system. We are equipped—though poorly—to cope with "ordinary" crime, with aberrational violent conduct. But law enforcement is not well designed to cope with political protests of the type we are now enduring. A policy of relative tolerance strongly offends a substantial public; so too does a policy of repression. The difficulty is that, whichever course is followed, law enforcement cannot win and stands discredited in the eyes of many. And that fact may have some indirect bearing on how we deal with ordinary crime.

The same may be said of the recent Supreme Court decisions that disturbed the majority of the members of Congress and, I am sure, their constituents. The concern of the Court was to make justice more equal. Aware of the fact that the experienced criminal or the affluent one knows his Constitutional rights, the Court has sought to lessen the gap between rich and poor and—often—white and black. To do so, it has imposed very strict and very difficult to administer standards concerning arrests, confessions, and the right to counsel.

There is a good deal of merit on both sides with respect to these decisions. Since law enforcement basically requires public support and confidence in its integrity and fairness, there is much to be said for ensuring that there is, in fact as well as theory, equal justice under law, especially if there are racial overtones to the inequality. (After all, our law-enforcement system from police through courts to corrections is predominantly white, and, in major cities, a large percentage of defendants are black.) On the other hand, it undoubtedly makes police administration more difficult. Psychologically, too, it is tough on policemen to be subjected to implied, and often unjustified, criticism at a time when crime is rising and their work is more dangerous and difficult.

The argument in support of these decisions is complex and difficult. The argument against them is simple. What is visible to an unsophisticated public is that, as a result of our "activist" Supreme Court, police are "handcuffed" in their fight against crime, and clearly guilty criminals go free. The more subtle benefits to law enforcement and our democratic society generally are either not observable or, as yet, not communicable.

What is nonsense is that these decisions have in any

way contributed to our growing crime rates. Whether one agrees with the Court or is critical of it, there should be no disagreement on that fact. Statistics demonstrate that less than 1 per cent of criminal prosecutions are adversely affected by Supreme Court decisions. Without them, our crime problem would be identical. At best, we would have had to find another scapegoat.

When President Johnson appointed his Crime Commission to study and make recommendations to him on the "challenge of crime," he did so in the consciousness of a growing fear of crime and a growing political issue. His hope was that this group of well-known citizens with the highest quality of professional help could depoliticize the problem. Despite the thoroughness of its study, the unanimity of its views, and the concreteness of its recommendations, it failed in this purpose. The debate on the Omnibus Crime Bill is a testimony to this failure.

The reasons for the failure lie in the background I have sketched and the strong emotions—skillfully played on by politicians—that the changes of this decade have wrought. We do have a deep political division in the United States, and the gap will be difficult to close. It will not be closed at all if we do not work hard to understand it.

There is a genuine fear of crime. It is strongly felt by rural white America, by blue-collar white America, and by those who live in modest suburbs. It is irrelevant to their emotions that, as a group, they probably have the least to fear from a growing crime rate. Ironically, it is also felt by the majority of black Americans who live in the ghetto and do have reason to fear crime—but who are silenced to a degree by the racial overtones ascribed to appeals for "law and order."

This predominantly middle-class white America probably adds up to a majority of Americans. Not only does it feel deeply about crime, but it is highly offended by pornography, by nudity, and by "long-haired kids." It is patriotic, has respect for the military, and supports Vietnam. It hunts and fishes—or used to do so—and it owns guns. It does not care much about "wire taps" or "bugs" or privacy. It may have a good deal of latent racial prejudice, but the majority probably is not—and certainly does not like to be called—racist. This group largely supported the 1964 and 1965 civil-rights acts. They deeply resent being classified as rednecks, which they are not.

I suppose it was almost inevitable that "law and order" got mixed up with civil rights. It had been, after all, the plea of the white segregationist. To compound the connection, "law and order" was also the catchword of Barry Goldwater—who voted against the 1964 Act—and George Wallace—the segregationist hero—in the 1964 and 1968 Presidential campaigns. It was, too, Senators McClellan and Ervin and Thurmond—fervent segregationists and strong critics of the Court's civil-rights decisions—who led the legislative battle to curb the Court on criminal procedure. And it was Dr. King who espoused the techniques of civil disobedience now utilized by young people in clear violation of clearly Constitutional laws.

My guess would be that most liberals, most representatives of national news media, most civil-rights leaders, and the majority of students at our best universities viewed Sheriff Clark's acts at Selma and the acts of the Chicago police force at the Democratic convention in similar fashion. Most of white middle-class America shared the public shock at Sheriff Clark's actions and thought the "kids" in Chicago got just what they deserved.

The story of the Omnibus Crime Bill is much more than a chronicle of Congressional idiosyncrasies and weaknesses. It is also the story of a failure by the Administration and by American intellectual leaders to communicate with this large segment of the American public. It cannot be done by ignoring their concerns or their fears. It cannot be done by saying or implying that they are motivated by racial bias.

Oddly enough, the one politician who did communicate —who did bridge the gap—was Robert F. Kennedy. We need men, like him, who can educate with feeling, to heal the divisions that the rhetoric of right and left is widening. One can only hope that this book will serve to remind other political leaders, and their counterparts in the intellectual world, of their failure and will encourage them to take up where Robert Kennedy left off.

*Armonk, N.Y.*
*July 9, 1969*

# THE FEAR OF CRIME

P ROBABLY the most distinctive characteristic of the successful politician is selective cowardice. The ordinary member of Congress, for example, spends much of his time twisting to meet this duty of office and turning to sidestep that one, all the while doing his best to make it appear that he is striding forward on a straight course that is set neither by favor nor by fear. What he tries most to avoid is carrying out any of his responsibilities in a way that might offend someone—almost anyone—for in political life it is the enemies, not the friends, one makes that count. As the seasoned politician also knows, it is usually the small step wrongly taken that sends one sprawling— say, the failure to do a favor for a constituent who has more political clout than one realizes, or the decision to vote for a minor provision of a minor bill which turns out to be against the vital interests of a group of determined constituents. Since senators and representatives are under such conflicting and relentless pressures that they cannot hope to avoid offending someone on just about every small issue that comes along, they generally try to make up for it by displeasing as few voters as possible on the big ones. More often than not, though, issues get big because members of Congress ignore them when they are small, avoid them as they grow, and attribute them to the wrong causes once they are unmanageably large. When this happens, the public, unaware that it has been misled by Congress about the nature of the problem, is almost certain to demand a resolution that is wrong. And Congress, tangled in deceit and weakened by timidity, is almost certain to grant it.

On June 6th, Congress enacted a law called the Omnibus Crime Control and Safe Streets Act of 1968, or, as it is more commonly known, the Crime Bill. Despite the views of all those who voted against it, many of those who voted for it, and most of those who didn't vote at all that the bill was a piece of demagoguery devised out of malevolence and enacted in hysteria, it was passed almost unanimously; in the House only seventeen members voted against it, and in the Senate only four. One senator who was necessarily absent when the roll was called but who announced that he would have voted against the measure had he been present was Wayne Morse, Democrat of Oregon, a former law-school dean who had been a member of Congress for twenty-three years; the bill, he told his colleagues during their deliberations on it, was "the most shocking and damaging piece of legislation I can remember being presented to the Senate." Other events of the spring—President Johnson's withdrawal as a candidate, two assassinations, and riots in a hundred cities—largely obscured the public's awareness of the bill, but to many outsiders who watched its progress final enactment of the measure surpassed any congressional folly within memory. "It will certainly damage this country severely, and it conceivably could destroy democracy as we know it," one of them said at the time. "At the very least, it constitutes a great leap toward a police state."

Early in 1967, the Commission on Law Enforcement and Administration of Justice, which the President had set up a year and a half before to study the causes of the alarming rise in the rate of crime in the United States and to propose remedies for it, submitted its report, entitled "The Challenge of Crime in a Free Society," to the White House. Like other crime studies, this one showed "that most crimes, wherever they are committed, are committed by boys and young men, and that most crimes, by whomever they are committed, are committed in cities." The facts were not particularly surprising, but to many readers the Commission's conclusions were. While it recommended immediate steps to upgrade the quality of the police and their methods, to revise outdated court systems, and to improve correctional techniques, it repeatedly stated that a lasting solution would require widespread recognition of basic matters that had long been overlooked or ignored and the development of a comprehensive program that would take as much money and understanding as the nation could muster. According to the Commission's report:

> It is with the young people and the slum dwellers who have been embittered by these painful social and economic pressures that the criminal justice system preponderantly deals. Society insists that individuals are responsible for their actions, and the criminal process operates on that assumption. However, society has not devised ways for ensuring that all its members have the ability to assume responsibility. It has let too many of them grow up untaught, unmotivated, unwanted. The criminal justice system has a great potential for dealing with individual instances of crime, but it was not designed to eliminate the conditions in which most crime breeds. It needs help. Warring on poverty, inadequate housing, and unemployment is warring on crime. A civil rights law is a law against crime. Money for schools is money against crime. Medical, psychiatric, and family-counseling services are services against crime. More broadly and most importantly every effort to improve life in America's "inner cities" is an effort against crime. A community's most enduring protection against crime is to right the wrongs and cure the illnesses that tempt men to harm their neighbors. . . . We will not have dealt effectively with crime until we have alleviated the conditions that stimulate it. To speak of controlling crime only in terms of the work of the police, the courts, and the correctional apparatus is to refuse to face the fact that widespread crime implies a widespread failure by society as a whole.

The Commission also pointed out, more or less in passing, that crime in this country was not on the rise quite as rampantly as most people thought. Much of the increase shown in statistics on crime in recent years has been due to a greater willingness on the part of the public to report crimes when they occur and a greater willingness on the part of public officials to keep complete records. Until a decade or two ago, for instance, the majority of crimes—those committed by the poor upon the poor in slums—were seldom reported, whereas increasing numbers of them are today. Further, current statistics include "crimes" that formerly never got on the books—youthful offenses like truancy, smoking, and running away from home, which make up a good portion of the half-million crimes committed every year by youngsters, and adult offenses like drunkenness, which make up one-third of all crimes. On the other hand, the Commission pointed out that in some areas an estimated nine crimes go unreported for every one that is reported, and it readily acknowledged that "the existence of crime, the talk about crime, the reports of crime, and the fear of crime have eroded the basic quality of life of many Americans."

The fear of crime, more than the fact of it, guaranteed that some kind of action would be taken, for the public demand had to be met. On February 6, 1967, the President took the first of many steps to meet it when he sent Congress a message on crime, in which he warned the legislators that "crime—and the fear of crime—has become a public malady," and went on to remind them of their "duty to seek its cure." His legislative recommendation, which he sent along with the message, was a bill called the Safe Streets and Crime Control Act of 1967—a title calculated to be politically irresistible. "It not only suggests that we're going to stop riots, muggings, and rapes but it also has a nostalgic quality—sort of a call back to the shady streets of 1910," an aide to one senator remarked. The bill provided federal aid to localities that set up approved programs for recruiting and training police, for modernizing equipment and reorganizing law-enforcement agencies, for developing advanced rehabilitation techniques and new ways to ease the return of ex-convicts to society, for modernizing court systems, and for setting up crime-prevention activities in schools, colleges, and welfare agencies. Since police power is the most jealously guarded of all state and local rights, the federal government was unable to do anything more than assist state and local law-enforcement agencies in improving the use of that power. The approach seemed unduly modest to many observers, but to the Administration this kind of help was vital if local efforts to control crime were to be effective. Back in 1961, a survey of three hundred police departments around the country had revealed that less than one per cent required any college training. Three years later, a pilot study ordered by the President showed that most criminals were mentally below average, which suggested that policemen who failed to stop or find them might not be much above it. As for police investigative technology, the police commissioner of Detroit had stated that until recent years there wasn't any. "Thirty years ago, they put a radio in a police car, and very little happened after that," he said. Furthermore, it was clear that the country's jail and prison system was little more than a giant crime school. Attorney General Ramsey Clark pointed out that three-fourths of those convicted of felonies had previously been convicted of misdemeanors, and that half of all the felons in prison were going to commit other felonies after release. "Corrections is a key, a very major part, of our total opportunity to reduce crime," he said. "If we cut the rate of recidivism in half—and science tells us we can—a major part of our crime will be eliminated." Nevertheless, matters were more or less at a standstill, he added, because "to date there has been no major national investment in corrections research." The most modest part of the Administration's proposal was its funding—limited because of the costs of the war in Vietnam—and the most the President could offer was fifty million dollars for the first year of the program and three hundred million dollars for the second year. Even the latter sum was paltry, considering that the annual cost of the country's entire system of criminal justice amounted to four billion dollars.

Members of Congress did not need the President's warning about the "public malady." They had just finished campaigns for election and re-election or annual fence-mending visits back home, and they knew the extent of their constituents' anxiety. It was greatest in and around large cities, but even in towns and villages where crime consisted of an occasional traffic violation or an arrest for drunkenness residents put crime at the top of their list of domestic concerns. Accordingly, no one in the capital doubted that Congress would give the President what he asked for, and when the bill was submitted in the Senate twenty-one members quickly lined up as co-sponsors. The measure, officially designated S. 917, was actually introduced by Senator John L. McClellan, Democrat of Arkansas, who was chairman of the Subcommittee on Criminal Laws and Procedures, which had been given jurisdiction over it. McClellan, who prides himself on being the Senate's fiercest crimebuster, evidently had little interest in the bill itself, as indicated by his stipulation that the records of his sponsorship of it include the words "by request." To him, it was pantywaist legislation. A stern and obdurate man with the mien of a Puritan patriarch who has just led his band ashore and now must get down to the real task of saving them from themselves, McClellan has scoffed at the notion that social unrest has social causes; he has sought not more laws but more freedom for police and prosecutors to use the laws they have—and more or less as they please. Those inside Congress and out who hoped that it would not approach the task of insuring domestic tranquillity simply by locking everybody up had little reason to believe that McClellan would provide the kind of leadership they had in mind. For one thing, his critics pointed out, most crime was committed in large cities, and McClellan was from a rural state, whose largest city had a population of a little over a hundred and twenty-five thousand. For another, most crime was committed by Negroes, and McClellan was a segregationist. And, finally, most crime was committed by the poor and disenfranchised, and McClellan had consistently voted to exclude them from the full functions of citizenship. "John thinks that the poor should not be listened to because they are not responsible members of society," one of his opponents on Capitol Hill has explained. "As he sees it, only the responsible people—that is, men of property—should have rights and run things." In the view of his harshest detractors, McClellan ultimately believed that the key to law and order was the one that was turned in the cell door of a criminal—or even a likely suspect—and then thrown away.

It soon became apparent that McClellan's chief interest in S. 917 lay in the opportunity it gave him to convene his subcommittee and hold hearings on the state of crime in general and his own favorite solutions to the problem in particular. He had already laid the groundwork. Informed beforehand of the President's intentions, McClellan had prepared and introduced two anti-crime measures of his own a couple of weeks before the White House sent S. 917 to him. The first of these, S. 674, went into the Senate hopper on January 24th and was widely expected to stay there. Among legal scholars, it was put down at the time as nothing more than another futile attack on the Supreme

Court, since it attempted to legislatively overturn two Supreme Court decisions, which, they held, could only be overturned by Constitutional amendment or by a subsequent ruling of the Court itself. The decisions McClellan was out to change were two landmark cases—Mallory v. United States (1957) and Miranda v. Arizona (1966)—which, along with several decisions handed down in the period between these two, reflected a growing concern on the part of the Court about abuses of defendants' Constitutional rights in criminal actions. The Mallory decision, by a unanimous Court, held that if an arresting officer failed to comply with the requirement laid down by the Federal Rules of Criminal Procedure that an arrested person be brought before a magistrate for a preliminary hearing "without unnecessary delay" a confession obtained during such a delay would be inadmissible in court. The purpose of the ruling, of course, was to prevent the police from obtaining confessions, valid or not, by the pressure of holding suspects incommunicado and questioning them intensively at inordinate length. Such methods, the Court held, were too often used when suspects were unaware of their specific rights or, indeed, that they had any rights. Following Mallory, the Court ruled on two cases that were to have an even greater effect on criminal law. The first decision was Gideon v. Wainwright, handed down in 1963 by a unanimous vote, which stipulated that if a defendant in a criminal case could not afford a lawyer the state had to provide one at his request—a reversal of a long-standing

22

Court ruling that free counsel was mandatory only in capital cases. That was followed, in 1964, by a five-to-four decision in the case of Escobedo v. Illinois, in which the Court stated that when a police investigation switched from "the exploratory to the accusatory stage" a suspect had to be allowed to consult a lawyer if he wished. Finally, in Miranda, Chief Justice Earl Warren, speaking for the majority in a five-to-four decision, stated that "when an individual is taken into custody or otherwise deprived of his freedom by the authorities and is subjected to questioning, the privilege against self-incrimination is jeopardized." As a safeguard, he went on, a suspect "must be warned prior to any questioning that he has the right to remain silent, that anything he says can be used against him in a court of law, that he has the right to the presence of an attorney, and that if he cannot afford an attorney, one will be appointed for him prior to any questioning if he so desires"; moreover, the Chief Justice added, "opportunity to exercise these rights must be afforded to him throughout the interrogation."

The essential concern of the Court in most of these cases centered on the role of confessions in our system of criminal law. Confessions are a favorite resort of law-enforcement officers, sometimes because they can't find the hard facts that would make a tight case, and other times because they are too lazy to go out and get them. Sir James Fitzjames Stephen, a prominent Victorian jurist, once remarked, "It is far pleasanter to sit comfortably in the shade rubbing red pepper into a poor devil's eyes than to go about in the sun hunting up evidence." That, of course, was the reason for the Fifth Amendment's protection against involuntary self-incrimination. If it is true, as Judge Walter V. Schaefer, of the Illinois Supreme Court, has held, that "the quality of a nation's civilization can be largely measured by the methods it uses in the enforcement of its criminal law," then the part played by confessions in that enforcement is critical. The threat to justice, and to society, posed by the careless use of confessions was perhaps best explained by John Henry Wigmore, for many years dean of the Faculty of Law at Northwestern University, in his famous ten-volume work, "Treatise on Evidence":

> Any system of administration which permits the prosecution to trust habitually to compulsory self-disclosure as a source of proof must itself suffer morally thereby. The inclination develops to rely mainly upon such evidence, and to be satisfied with an incomplete investigation of the other sources. The exercise of the power to extract answers begets a forgetfulness of the just limitations of that power. The simple and peaceful process of questioning breeds a readiness to resort to bullying and to physical force and torture. If there is a right to an answer, there soon seems to be a right to the expected answer—that is, to a confession of guilt. Thus, the legitimate use grows into the unjust abuse; ultimately, the innocent are jeopardized by the encroachments of a bad system.

McClellan and his followers were quick to point out

that the use of the third degree, while once the general practice followed by police in this country, had fallen off to the point where it was rarely found. To be sure, it had decreased markedly—largely because of Supreme Court reversals of convictions where there was any sign of it— but in the opinion of Chief Justice Warren in the Miranda case it was still "sufficiently widespread to be the object of concern." Of far greater concern, he continued, was the simultaneous growth of the sophisticated use of psychological pressures on suspects during interrogation, which had led him to conclude that "the blood of the accused is not the only hallmark of an unconstitutional inquisition." To illustrate this, he cited some instructions taken from several police manuals on interrogation. One suggested that all interviews with suspects be conducted in police headquarters or at least a place of the investigator's choice, and explained, "The subject should be deprived of every psychological advantage. In his own home he may be confident, indignant, or recalcitrant. He is more keenly aware of his rights and more reluctant to tell of his indiscretions of criminal behavior within the walls of his own home. Moreover, his family and other friends are nearby, their presence lending moral support. In his own office, the investigator possesses all the advantages. The atmosphere suggests the invincibility of the forces of the law." Investigators, once within the walls that they found as reassuring as the suspect found frightening, were advised to try out various "tricks," such as assuring the suspect that they knew the basic truth and wanted only some small details filled in; sympathizing with the suspect until they had convinced him that the victim or society was really at fault and he was morally guiltless; and persuading the suspect to claim that he had committed the crime in self-defense, and then persuading him to divulge some seemingly insignificant fact to make a plea of self-defense impossible. If all this failed, the investigator was advised that he "must interrogate steadily and without relent, leaving the subject no prospect of surcease." If this also failed, still other means were at hand. One was to put a suspect in a lineup and have a coached witness pick him out as the criminal; afterward the suspect was to be asked about details of the crime, as if the question of guilt were all settled. Another was to employ what one manual called a "reverse lineup," in which the suspect "is identified by several fictitious witnesses or victims who associated him with different offenses." After that, the manual concluded, "it is expected that the subject will become desperate and confess to the offense under investigation in order to escape from the false accusations."

Critics of the Miranda ruling complained that it brought lawyers into criminal proceedings very near the start—that is, when suspects asked for their help. And, as Senator McClellan said, "it is widely known that counsel will advise the suspect to make no statement at all." In the Escobedo case, Justice Arthur Goldberg addressed himself to this point in the majority opinion. "No system worth preserving should have to *fear* that if an accused is permitted to consult with a lawyer, he will become aware of, and exercise, these rights," he wrote. "If the exercise of constitutional rights will thwart the effectiveness of a system of law enforcement, then there is something very wrong with that system." That lawyers invariably advise silence is, as McClellan contended, widely known—by members of crime syndicates, professional criminals, anyone who has spent time in prison, and reasonably enlightened citizens. But it is not so widely known by those McClellan seemed to be after—the poor and the ignorant, most of whom have seen little sign in their lives that they possess any rights at all. "The defendant who does not ask for counsel is the very defendant who most needs counsel," Chief Justice Warren said in Miranda. "The need for counsel in order to protect the [Fifth Amendment] privilege exists for the indigent as well as the affluent. In fact, were we to limit these constitutional rights to those who can retain an attorney, our decisions today would be of little significance. The cases before us, as well as the vast majority of confession cases with which we have dealt in the past, involve those unable to retain counsel."

It was clear that the Chief Justice expected the Miranda ruling to set off a round of protests by policemen and prosecutors, and to create fresh demands that Congress take steps to control the Court—which seemed to happen now whenever the Court announced an opinion—for he warned, "Where rights secured by the Constitution are involved, there can be no rule-making or legislation which would abrogate them." McClellan was not intimidated by this statement; neither was he put off by the weight of juridical opinion throughout the nation's history, which unanimously affirmed the role of the Supreme Court as final arbiter over what the Constitution and the Bill of Rights mean; nor, finally, was he concerned about upsetting the delicate balance that keeps the three branches of our government separate and upright. Perhaps none of these considerations made him pause because he was convinced, like everyone else at the time, that his bill had no chance. "John can be an awful demagogue when he wants to, and this was one time when he wanted to," a fellow-senator remarked later. "The bill was just a way of lambasting the Court and getting some publicity for making a good try. Of course, if anything came of it, so much the better."

S. 674 was less than a page long. "In any criminal prosecution brought by the United States or by the District of Columbia, a confession . . . shall be admissible in evidence if it is voluntarily given," it declared. That was enough to repeal Miranda in all federal cases and, by inevitable extension as state legislatures followed suit, in all other cases, too. In sum, it returned matters to the guideline that had traditionally been followed when a question about the validity of a confession was raised—namely, whether it was offered without coercion of any kind. The bill went on to instruct trial judges to determine whether confessions were voluntary or involuntary by measuring them against such factors as whether the length of time from arrest to arraignment, if the confession was given in between the two, was inordinate; whether the defendant knew the nature of the offense he was charged with; whether he was told or knew that he could remain silent and that anything he said might be held against him; whether he was told that he had a right to counsel; and whether counsel was present when he was questioned and when he confessed. While all of these questions were to be considered by the trial judge, he was bound by none of them.

The second part of S. 674 disposed of Mallory, by stating that in federal courts a confession was not "inadmissible solely because of delay in bringing such person before a commissioner or other officer empowered to commit persons charged with offenses" as long as the trial judge found that the confession had been given voluntarily and it had been left to the jury to weigh in its over-all deliberations. In other words, a suspect could be held indefinitely. This part of the bill threw out Rule 5 of the Federal Rules of Criminal Procedure, but since those rules had been devised by the Supreme Court with the assent of Congress, McClellan's supporters argued, it was perfectly proper for Congress to withdraw its assent and revise the rules. Some others, however, held that a revision of the sort McClellan proposed would violate the Constitution, because it abused the Fifth Amendment prohibition against self-incrimination and the Fourteenth Amendment insistence on due process. Rule 5, they pointed out, had been an effort to elaborate and define Constitutionally based rights, and it could only be broadened, not narrowed.

"The reason the police cannot stop crime is the Court decisions," Senator McClellan tirelessly repeated, in one form or another. And his opponents tirelessly responded that the contention was, in the words of former Attorney General Nicholas deB. Katzenbach, "unutterable nonsense." The hardened criminal already knew his rights, they said, and the ordinary desperado would hardly wait for a signal from Washington before he robbed, mugged, or raped someone. A few people found the charges and countercharges irrelevant, because in their opinion McClellan's actions had nothing to do with crime but everything to do with a conspiratorial attack on the Supreme Court. As this group saw it, McClellan was using the growing unpopularity of the Court's decisions in criminal cases—much of which he and his followers had created in the first place—to give it a thrashing for its decisions in civil-rights cases, particularly the 1954 decision to desegregate public schools. Evidence for this theory grew apace. First was the list of S. 674's co-sponsors—all arch-conservative Southerners, along with their most faithful ally in the North, Roman L. Hruska, Republican of Nebraska, a man who has apparently long lived with the harrowing fear that somewhere someone may be helping the helpless. Then, shortly before McClellan convened the Subcommittee on Criminal Laws and Procedures for hearings on S. 917,

S. 674, and more than a dozen other anti-crime bills await-
ing action by the Senate, James O. Eastland, the chairman of
the subcommittee's parent body, the Committee on the
Judiciary, unexpectedly expanded the subcommittee by
adding one of the Senate's more liberal members, Edward
M. Kennedy, and two of its most reactionary members,
Strom Thurmond, the Democrat-turned-Dixiecrat-turned-
Republican from South Carolina, and himself. The lineup
put McClellan, Eastland, Hruska, Thurmond, and Sam J.
Ervin, Jr., Democrat of North Carolina, on the far right;
Kennedy and Philip A. Hart, Democrat of Michigan,
slightly to the left; and Hugh Scott, Republican of Pennsylvania, in the center. Another piece of evidence support-
ing the conspiracy theory was a move by Senator Ervin, a
few days before the hearings opened, to file a resolution
proposing a Constitutional amendment to restrict the
powers of the Supreme Court. In effect, the amendment
would eliminate the Court's authority to review confessions in federal and state criminal cases as long as the
trial courts involved affirmed the voluntary character of
the confessions. This would accomplish the same thing
as McClellan's bill, except that it would extend the limitation on the Court directly to state cases. It also indicated
that Ervin, the Senate's leading expert on Constitutional
law, believed that McClellan's attempt to curb the Court
by way of legislation might well be un-Constitutional.

"It is quite probable that these hearings and the bills we

will be considering will mark the turning point in the struggle against lawlessness in this nation," McClellan said in his opening statement when the hearings began, on March 7, 1967, which happened to be in the middle of Law Enforcement Week. It was an ominous prophecy, and it was made more ominous a few minutes later when Senator Ervin announced that he had come to a turning point of his own and had concluded that Congress had the power, after all, to enact legislation along the lines of what he had proposed in his Constitutional amendment. "I am, therefore, introducing today a bill which would re-move the jurisdiction of the Supreme Court and inferior federal appellate courts to reverse or otherwise disturb a ruling by a federal trial court admitting a confession as voluntarily made if such ruling is supported by any compe-tent evidence," he said. "The bill would also similarly limit the jurisdiction of federal courts to review, reverse, or otherwise disturb a ruling by a state trial court that a con-fession is voluntary and admissible if such ruling has been upheld by the highest appellate court of that state."

Of course, if there was to be a concerted attack on the Court, a Constitutional amendment would have been of little help, immediately anyway, since it would require the approval of two-thirds of the members of the House and the Senate and ratification by three-fourths of the states— a long, arduous, and chancy business at best. Legislation to the same end would be far quicker and easier. If it should subsequently be knocked down as un-Constitutional, that outcome would increase the numbers and ire of the Court's opponents, and thereby perhaps intimidate both the Court and any President who was about to appoint a new justice; at the same time, it would make the passage of a Constitutional amendment more likely later on. Among the co-sponsors of Ervin's bill were two subcommittee members, Thurmond and Eastland, along with such Southern Democrats as Ernest F. Hollings, of South Carolina; Robert C. Byrd, of West Virginia; B. Everett Jordan, of North Carolina; Harry F. Byrd, of Virginia; Lister Hill, of Alabama; Allen J. Ellender, of Louisiana; Herman E. Talmadge, of Georgia; and Russell B. Long, of Louisiana, the Majority Whip. At the Northern end of the axis were right-wing Republicans like Bourke B. Hickenlooper, of Iowa; Paul J. Fannin, of Arizona; Wallace F. Bennett, of Utah; and Clifford P. Hansen, of Wyoming. None of them came from states with the kind of great urban centers where most of the nation's crime is committed.

Senator McClellan is known as the most adroit committee chairman on the Hill when it comes to generating publicity for something that he is concerned about, or that he wants to appear to be concerned about. A former rural prosecutor of the jury-rail-thumping variety, he has always made great use of simplicity in conducting Senate hearings. Characteristically, he has stuck to one main point and one side of that point—his. In this case, his point was the same one that he had been making all along—that decisions of the Supreme Court endangered the nation's stability. But he also said, "I want to get the other side of it and see what can be presented in opposition to these bills. I want to get the most forceful arguments that can be made against them in this record." To accomplish this, he invited fifty-odd witnesses to testify, only half a dozen of whom opposed his viewpoint, and he inserted in the record scores of letters, editorials, and statements favorable to his position, with only a handful opposed. Not one of the witnesses and correspondents was a criminologist, a leading professor of law, or an expert on the Constitution. Instead, most of them were police officers and prosecutors, with a few judges who agreed with McClellan thrown in.

To keep his viewpoint sharply in focus, McClellan relied on repeated use of several currently popular phrases—chiefly, that members of the Supreme Court and others in high places, by "coddling criminals" and "handcuffing the police," had dispatched "the depraved to roam the streets at will" and "prey on the innocent." No one seems to know for sure where these phrases originated, but it would appear that they gained currency through constant reiteration by police officials and prosecutors who were bewildered and angered by the way the Court kept changing the rules in the middle of the game. In time, the clichés began to appear in newspapers and on television—usually in interviews with police officers and prosecutors who were under pressure to explain why they were not dealing more effectively with crime—and then were taken up and pushed by right-wing spokesmen as part of their general attack on "the Warren Court." With increasing frequency, the phrases began to pop up in letters written to members of Congress, until today a perusal of the mail that any of them receives reveals that nine-tenths of the voters who complain about "crime in the streets" complain in these terms. Those who are fond of the sound of the words apparently do not stop to ask what they mean, for one would be hard put to it to explain why a justice of the Supreme Court or any other high government official would want to be unduly lenient with those who despoil society or unduly harsh with those who protect it. In any event, it is increasingly clear that such clichés can have a monumental effect on the political life of the nation. Their repetition thousands of times a day has brought a great many people to the point where they seriously doubt that the government's interest is the same as their own.

McClellan's charge that the Miranda decision had released criminals who had confessed their guilt was true, but not in the way he made it appear. Sometimes by implication, but more often directly, he charged that the ruling had opened the doors of the nation's penitentiaries and let loose hordes of vicious criminals simply because they had confessed to what he called "heneous" crimes without benefit of counsel. Actually, a week after handing down the Miranda decision, the Supreme Court, in the case of Johnson v. New Jersey, ruled that Miranda applied only to cases tried after June 13, 1966, the date of the Miranda decision. In terms of retroactivity, this involved only cases in which the prosecution might still be intending to submit arraigned but untried defendants' confessions in court. But even this limited form of retroactivity gave opponents of the Court a basis for attack that the public could easily grasp and would inevitably resent. By far the most widely publicized example in this category involved a man in Brooklyn who had confessed to murdering his common-law wife and her five children. Because the state's case was largely based on his confession, which had been obtained without the presence of a lawyer, and because he had not been tried before June 13, 1966, the court was obliged to release him. "I say it is a sad commentary on our system of justice when a man can murder his wife and five little children, and admit it, and then be turned loose on a technicality because somebody didn't tell him he was entitled to a lawyer," McClellan said at the hearings. "I think it is tragic."

Senator Hart, who approved of the Miranda decision but had doubts about its retroactive extension, agreed. "It *is* tragic," he said. But he went on to point out that while Johnson v. New Jersey had created a number of regrettable situations because the police were held to a standard that they hadn't known about at the time they made arrests, it applied only to a limited number of cases—far more limited than McClellan constantly suggested—and that once they were disposed of there would be no confusion about the rules as they were applied to arrests made after June 13, 1966. As for legal technicalities, he told Mc-

Clellan, "it is a technicality that you couldn't use a rack," and he added that "these are all technicalities intended to protect substantive rights." McClellan ignored the point and continued to hammer away at the use of technicalities to release "self-confessed murderers and rapists." Finally, Hart reminded him that the entire Bill of Rights was nothing but technicalities. It was not the rules that were at fault, he said, but, rather, those who failed to observe them.

Another matter that McClellan dwelt on at length was that criminals who had been let off on such technicalities often took the first opportunity to commit another crime —as happened with both Danny Escobedo, who was subsequently convicted of possessing and selling heroin and sentenced to twenty-two years in prison, and Andrew R. Mallory, who was subsequently convicted of burglary and aggravated assault and sentenced to eleven and a half to twenty-three years in prison. McClellan did not dwell at all on the later history of Ernesto Miranda, who was retried on the original kidnapping and rape charges, this time without the use of his confession, again found guilty, and sent back to prison to serve out the same sentence that he had received the first time. One of McClellan's witnesses, Judge Laurence T. Wren, of the Superior Court of Arizona, who presided at Miranda's second trial, testified at some length during the hearings. After recounting how he had heard Miranda confess again—during a court interrogation while the jury was excluded—the Judge turned to the matter of the jury's verdict of guilty and said of it, "This was unfortunate, because it lends credence to the Supreme Court's statement that without the confession to police there was still adequate evidence." Even McClellan's supporters had not expected to hear a judge express regret that a guilty man had not gone free, since his release would have embarrassed the Supreme Court.

The most prominent of the policemen who felt that they had been handcuffed by the Court and who appeared at the hearings to talk about it was Quinn Tamm, executive director of the International Association of Chiefs of Police. "I am of the firm opinion that the majority of the decent people of this country have had about enough of a judicial system which allows criminals to roam the streets and commit vicious, depraved acts time after time after time," he said. "I believe our citizens are fully aware of the situation, and I predict that if there is not a turning point reached soon toward more realistic Supreme Court decisions, we are going to witness one of the greatest surges of outraged citizenship that we have ever seen." Tamm went on to advise President Johnson on how he should fill the Court vacancy soon to be created by Justice Tom Clark's retirement—with a conservative, Tamm said, in order that the Court might be kept from becoming "even more one-sided in its interpretive philosophies." To demonstrate the widespread support for his views among the sixty-five hundred members of his association, he had earlier informed them of McClellan's efforts and urged them to write the Senator to express their support. Dozens of them did, and McClellan dutifully put their letters in the record—apparently unread, for though all of them were meant to buttress his position, some inadvertently kicked out the props. One letter, from the chief of police in an Oregon town called The Dalles, stated, "We had two murders the latter part of 1966 and were successful in getting convictions only because our District Attorney is insistent that all cases be handled with the proper preliminary warnings and chances to call an attorney." A fair number of the other letters revealed that their authors thought the Court had outlawed the use of confessions in trials altogether, and still others thought that it had forbidden even their expression unless a lawyer was by a suspect's side. "This era reveals that a person is not allowed to unburden his troubles or cleanse his soul and conscience without being accompanied by a lawyer," the chief of police of Southampton, Pennsylvania, wrote, and added that this clearly violated the right of free speech. Of course, nothing in the Miranda ruling prevented a suspect who was offered legal counsel from refusing it—and many suspects did—or from ignoring a lawyer's advice to remain silent and confessing to his heart's content. There was no record of how many policemen around the country had shared this sort of misunderstanding and let chargeable offenders go.

One of the few law-enforcement officials who expressly disagreed with McClellan and Tamm was Ray Girardin, the police commissioner of Detroit. McClellan pressed him to concede that the Miranda case had hurt the efforts of his department, but Girardin stated—and repeated as he was pressed—that he didn't know of a single case that had been affected by it. "I certainly don't have the impression that we have a revolving door at police headquarters," he said. Although the country's district attorneys were generally as strong in praise of McClellan's work as the policemen were, again there were a few dissenters. For example, Evelle J. Younger, the district attorney of Los Angeles County, who was unable to attend the hearings but sent in a memorandum, reported that his department had conducted a study after the Miranda ruling was handed down and that, aside from the problems presented by its retroactive nature, "insofar as we are able to observe from the prosecutors' viewpoint, this decision has not materially affected our ability to convict." Michael Dillon, the district attorney of Erie County, New York, which includes Buffalo and contains more than a million people, told the subcommittee that he was familiar with Younger's study and that he agreed with its conclusions. This led to a deep scowl on McClellan's part and the following exchange:

> SENATOR MCCLELLAN: Let me ask you, do you think the Miranda decision strengthens law enforcement in this country?
> MR. DILLON: I think the Miranda decision, Senator, represents a balance between the interests of law enforcement and the rights of individuals. Senator, all people in

our society are not as fortunate as you or as I am fortunate. My experience is that we hold people sometimes in jail, young people in jail, for days at a time with a complete lack of concern of the parents, if they do live in homes where parents live together, a complete lack of concern in many instances on the part of the community or other agencies as to where these young people are or what they are doing. . . . This would not happen, Senator, if others in the more affluent society were arrested under similar circumstances. There would be a lawyer there immediately, there would be a brother or a sister or a mother or a father there immediately. . . . So I find no objection, Senator, with telling those who have engaged in criminal activities that anything they say may be used against them because others in our society know that. I have no quarrel with telling them that they have a right to remain silent, because others more affluent in our society already know that. Nor do I find any quarrel with telling them that they have a right to an attorney, and that if they cannot afford an attorney, one will be provided for them. Therefore, I do not quarrel with the Miranda decision.

Dillon also agreed with Younger that "many of these seemingly restrictive decisions" of the Supreme Court would "contribute directly to a more effective, efficient, and professional level of law enforcement" by compelling the police to develop and use sharper skills. Commissioner Girardin had made the same point, and so did Lawrence Speiser, the spokesman for the American Civil Liberties Union, who was allowed to testify on the last day of the hearings. "Recent rulings on confessions have not so much restricted police procedure as they have improved it," he told the subcommittee. "Knowing their procedures will be closely scrutinized in court, police are doing a more thorough job of investigation, relying on careful research rather than tainted or questionable confessions or searches. As watchman over police practices, the Court is fulfilling an historic role."

Time and again during the hearings, Senator McClellan raised the issue of the damage being done to the morale of the police when the Court undid their work. Dillon, for one, was in full agreement that this had "a tremendously adverse impact." For a moment, McClellan brightened, but then he lapsed back into his customary dour attitude as Dillon went on to say that police morale would finally be raised only by better training, more advanced equipment, and higher pay, and added that once these improvements were made the police would be able to function effectively and contentedly within the new rules. But McClellan stuck to his argument that the rules imposed too much of a burden on the police, who were trying diligently and fairly to carry out their duties. Finally, Senator Hart, an unfailingly polite man, broke in:

> Some of these decisions cause a lot of trouble, and it is the kind of trouble that no police state ever suffers from. The people of this country react with abhorrence when they read of people who have to live in a country where they knock on the door in the middle of the night, take the man away, not to a magistrate but to some jail. We like to

think, Isn't it nice that we don't do things like that? Let's be sure that we don't begin to move in that direction by overreaction. The right to keep quiet, that is the right of the poor man as well as the rich fellow, and the right to a lawyer and to a phone booth at least to get the lawyer right away, that is everybody's right. To be told promptly on arraignment of what it is that you are charged with, that is a right. And none of these are new rights. There is nothing new about this. What I sense may be new is a series of decisions by which the Court seeks to insure that those rights which wealthy Americans have always enjoyed will be extended to all Americans.

That was the long form of the more or less standard reply that Hart was to make again and again in the campaign against the anti-Court bill. When he didn't have time, he used a short form: "The Bill of Rights was not written to make things easier for the police."

McClellan was less interested in the substance of Hart's reasoning than in its implication. "I fail to see where we were moving toward a police state in this country prior to these decisions," he said testily. Later, he went out of his way to make it clear that he considered himself the guardian against a police state, not its promoter, and hinted darkly at what the opposition would do to him if it could—as, for example, in a colloquy with one of his admirers, Aaron Koota, then the district attorney of Brooklyn and now a judge on the New York State Supreme Court:

SENATOR MCCLELLAN: Has it occurred to you, if I may

interrupt, that those who today disagree with the President, and the Commander-in-Chief, as to the conduct of the war assert the right to dissent?

MR. KOOTA: Precisely.

SENATOR MCCLELLAN: I wonder if some of them will accord to us the right to dissent and make our position known with respect to some things that are happening to this country from within.

MR. KOOTA: I am very dubious about that, Mr. Chairman.

SENATOR MCCLELLAN: I wonder.

MR. KOOTA: I wonder.

Other witnesses needed no prompting from the Chairman. "I enthusiastically approve of Senate Bill 674," Judge Michael A. Musmanno, of the Pennsylvania Supreme Court, told the subcommittee, and proved it by devoting most of his testimony to metaphorical attacks on the Miranda decision. For the first ten or fifteen minutes, they were medical. The Court's "prescription," he said, did not "coincide with the nature of the malignant disease, and, in consequence, many cancerous criminals and pestilential psychopaths are stalking the streets of the nation, polluting the communities through which they move," because the police "failed to administer . . . the paregoric prescribed in Miranda." Moving on to belabor the decision in soothsaying, nautical, acrobatic, and architectural terms, Musmanno finally reached the high point of his brief against the Court when he sought to illustrate the dangers of the Miranda ruling by applying it to Patrolman J. D. Tippit as he confronted Lee Harvey Oswald after the assassination of President Kennedy. His voice quivering with emotion, Musmanno declaimed, "Imagine that policeman saying, if he could talk to Oswald, 'Before you speak, I want you to know that you can have an attorney. Before you speak, or I can listen to you, I want you to know that if you don't have an attorney, we must get you one and we dare not question you.' This man, armed with a pistol and rifle and heaven knows what other weapons. That is what the Miranda case would have provided for in that disgraceful, shameful page of our history." Of course, it would have provided for nothing of the sort. Nothing in the decision would have prevented Tippit from taking whatever steps were necessary to protect himself, or from taking the suspect into custody. Nothing would have prevented Oswald from talking endlessly to Tippit. Nothing would have prevented Tippit from listening to Oswald and hearing his confession, except that it could not be used in evidence unless the proper warning had been given or, after it was given, Oswald decided to repeat his confession. Otherwise, of course, any criminal could avoid standing trial simply by blurting out a confession before the police had a chance to warn him. Even Senator McClellan looked somewhat embarrassed as Judge Musmanno completed his testimony.

One issue raised repeatedly at the hearings concerned the effect of Miranda on the willingness of suspects to confess. District Attorney Koota, for instance, testified that in his jurisdiction around ten per cent of all suspects held in serious felonies had refused to make statements in the days before the Miranda rule, whereas afterward the percentage rose to forty-one. Across the river in Manhattan, District Attorney Frank S. Hogan reported that prior to the Miranda rule fifty-one per cent of defendants in all felony cases except homicide had refused to confess, whereas in the six months after it eighty-five per cent of them had refused. Arlen Specter, district attorney of Philadelphia, said that before Miranda less than thirty-two per cent of all suspects arrested in that city had refused to give statements to the police, and that afterward fifty-nine per cent of them had refused. Putting aside the discrepancies and concentrating instead on the common decline in the number of statements, McClellan devoted a substantial part of the testimony that he took—better than twelve hundred pages before it was all over—to showing that fewer suspects admitted their guilt after Miranda than did before. Of course, this was just what the Supreme Court had intended, for if those who were already informed about their rights used them, those who became informed could be expected to use them, too. If the exercise of civil liberties weakened the police, McClellan's opponents stated, the solution was more skillful investigation, not dubious interrogation.

Although it was frequently alleged that the police had been hampered by Miranda, the decision clearly had no effect whatever on their dealings with several classes of criminals. "A hardened criminal never told us anything anyway," Commissioner Girardin explained, and he went on to say that this was true even of youngsters. "We have rapists at fourteen, stickup men with a gun at the same age," he said. "They won't tell us anything, and they haven't for many years." Neither would members of crime syndicates like the Cosa Nostra, he and other law-enforcement officials testified. McClellan was particularly fond of making this point himself, and of leading witnesses to make it for him, even though it demonstrated that he hoped through his bill to prevent the only people left who didn't know their rights—the ignorant, the poor, the unwary—from learning them.

Those who believed that there was a conspiracy in the Senate to enact a piece of obviously un-Constitutional legislation that the Supreme Court might knock down, and thereby create what one senator called "the dismal prospect of yet another self-defeating round of police frustration and public dissatisfaction with the courts," soon concluded that a second bill introduced by McClellan and discussed in the hearings was directed to the same purpose. This measure, which he submitted the day after S. 674 was submitted, dealt with the interception of communications by means of electrical (wiretapping) and electronic (bugging) devices. It was generally agreed that some sort of legislation was overdue, for as matters stood there was a clutter of conflicting laws on the subject—

private wiretapping and bugging constituted felonies in seven states, for example, but were not even crimes in forty-three states—and neither Congress nor the Supreme Court had done much to put things in order. The sole federal statute governing wiretapping was the Federal Communications Act of 1934, Section 605 of which stated that "no person not being authorized by the sender shall intercept any communication and divulge or publish the existence, contents, substance, purport, effect, or meaning of such intercepted communication to any person." The law appeared to be rigorously strict, but law-enforcement officials around the country had quickly realized that while it prohibited anyone from divulging what he had learned by way of a wiretap, it said nothing about his learning it. In other words, it seemed to be all right to use wiretaps to uncover leads as long as the information obtained wasn't revealed in court. (Ultimately, of course, many prosecutors succumbed to the temptation to use the information in court while concealing its source.)

The Supreme Court's first word on the subject came in 1928, when it ruled that intercepting telephone messages and using them as evidence did not constitute an unreasonable search and seizure, forbidden under the Fourth Amendment, since there was no trespass into Constitutionally protected areas and no seizure of anything tangible. In opinions handed down over the years, the Court ruled, variously, that evidence and even leads (called "tainted fruits of the forbidden tree") obtained by way of wiretapping were inadmissible in federal courts; that the restriction applied to intrastate as well as interstate calls as long as the carrier's over-all operations crossed a state line; that only a party to a tapped conversation could object to its use as evidence; that a third party could listen to a telephone conversation with the permission of one of the parties to it; and that state officials could divulge evidence gained by wiretapping in state but not federal courts. When the Court got around to bugging, it ruled—again in a number of different cases—that the process was un-Constitutional if it amounted to an unauthorized physical invasion of the defendant's property or the premises he occupied temporarily (a sensitive microphone placed on the outside of the wall of a motel room occupied by a suspect was all right, but a "spike mike" inserted in a heating duct inside a suspect's house was not); that a police informer could be wired for sound that would be transmitted to police officers located elsewhere; that a federal agent could use a tape recorder concealed on his person while talking with a suspect who knew that he was an agent but did not know that he was bugged; and, in a decision delivered shortly before McClellan introduced his bill, that conversations did come under the prohibition against unreasonable search and seizure after all, and were governed by the same restrictions that applied to search warrants, which involved giving a judge a specific description of the crime that had been or was being committed and a specific description of the evidence that would prove it.

In his State of the Union Message delivered before a joint session of Congress on January 10, 1967, President Johnson had said, "We should protect what Justice Brandeis called the 'right most valued by civilized men'—the right to privacy. We should outlaw all wiretapping—public and private—wherever and whenever it occurs, except when the security of this nation itself is at stake, and only then with the strictest governmental safeguards." On February 8th, an Administration bill to accomplish this was introduced in the Senate by Edward V. Long, Democrat of Missouri, who had already conducted lengthy hearings on the subject in his Subcommittee on Administrative Practice and Procedure and who intended to hold a good many more. The Administration's bill—numbered S. 928 and called the Right of Privacy Act—was co-sponsored by twenty-two senators. This time, McClellan was not among them. As he saw it, the bill was another piece of legislative mollycoddling, and he refused to have anything to do with it. Instead, he pressed for passage of his own measure, S. 675, which he introduced on January 25th. Like the Administration's bill, S. 675 prohibited private tapping and bugging, regulated the manufacture and distribution of devices by which tapping and bugging could be accomplished, and permitted the President to use either form of surveillance to safeguard the security of the nation against foreign enemies. But, unlike the Administration's bill, S.

675 also gave the President the authority "to take such measures as he deems necessary to protect the United States against the overthrow of the government by force or other unlawful means, or against any other clear and present danger to the structure or existence of the government." Finally, the bill allowed any federal Assistant Attorney General (with the approval of the Attorney General and a federal judge) or any state attorney general or local district attorney (with the approval of a judge in his jurisdiction) to tap a telephone or plant a bug if there was reason to believe that it would produce evidence about any crime punishable by a year in prison which had been committed, was being committed, or was about to be committed. Officials could listen in on any conversation on a suspect's telephone or premises for up to forty-five days, and could get twenty-day renewals indefinitely as long as a judge approved.

Once again, policemen and prosecutors appeared at the hearings to speak out for McClellan's bill, which would regulate, and in effect greatly expand, the use of wire-tapping and bugging. Orlando W. Wilson, former superintendent of police in Chicago, stated that "organized crime poses a greater threat to the American way of life than even Communism," which no one disagreed with, and claimed that "we will make no substantial inroads against organized crime without the use of electronic surveillance," which several people disagreed with. One of them, Commissioner Girardin, said he didn't see that electronic surveillance would do much good. "I can conceive of it working [with] the unwary," he explained. "But criminals certainly are sophisticated enough, I believe, not to discuss their nefarious acts over the telephone." If they weren't that sophisticated, others remarked, they would become so very soon after a bill like S. 675 was enacted, leaving the police with a great deal of equipment and no one to listen in on except perhaps some personal or political enemies and, when that palled, on anyone whose activities sounded interesting. For this reason, Girardin expressed grave fears about "wiretapping unless it is very, very carefully controlled." When asked why he felt this way, he replied, "Because in my experience people have become overzealous in the use of wiretaps—legally or illegally—and this invasion, I think, is a very dangerous situation."

Frank Hogan, the chief spokesman for big-city district attorneys, again supported McClellan's approach, on the ground that tapping and bugging constituted "the single most valuable and effective weapon in the arsenal of law enforcement." To support this contention, he stated that without it there would have been no way of convicting such underworld figures as Lucky Luciano, Lepke Buchalter, Socks Lanza, Johnny Dio, and Frank Carbo. Wiretapping had been legal in New York State since 1938 and bugging since 1958 ("pursuant to court order and under proper safeguards," Hogan said), and over those respective periods an average of only sixty-six wiretaps and nineteen bugs had been installed each year, with court permission, in Manhattan. Hogan cited the Crime Commission's support of tapping and bugging in organized-crime cases, but he did not mention that the Commission had called for far stricter safeguards than S. 675 contained. Attorney General Ramsey Clark found even the Crime Commission's guarded approach insupportable. "Public safety will not be found in wiretapping," he said. "Security is to be found in excellence in law enforcement, in courts, and in corrections. . . . Nothing so mocks privacy as the wiretap and electronic surveillance. They are incompatible with a free society." Going on to say that "only the most urgent need can justify" such intrusions, he charged that people like Hogan had failed to make a case, "much less meet the heavy burden of proof our values require," and demanded, "Where is the evidence that this is an efficient police technique?"

Clark reluctantly expressed support of the provision that the President be given the authority to order wiretapping and electronic eavesdropping when the nation's security was threatened, but insisted on the most rigorous safeguards to insure that the authority was not abused. Senator Hart argued that McClellan's bill offered a despotically inclined President enough power to abuse just about anyone in sight. On a President's own motion, Hart explained, he could declare—apparently to himself—that members of a left-wing or a right-wing political group, participants in a national labor dispute, draft protesters, civil-rights demonstrators, or any kind of political dissenters constituted "a clear and present danger to the structure or existence of the government," and from that moment on he could listen to everything they said. That sounded bad enough, Hart said, but the rest of the bill was worse, for it created "an indiscriminate dragnet," which would pick up conversations not only of a suspect but of anyone who happened to speak to him—and, if the dragnet was extended zealously, of anyone who happened to speak to someone remotely connected with him. In a statement submitted for the record of the hearings, the A.C.L.U. charged that S. 675 clearly violated the Fourth Amendment's prohibition against "unreasonable searches and seizures." "If there was any one abuse with which the framers of our Constitution were concerned, it was with the general warrants and the writs of assistance which authorized general exploratory searches," it explained. "To prevent this, the founders required the search and seizure to be limited to specifically listed items. This requirement cannot possibly be complied with where wiretapping and bugging are concerned, for no such limitation is possible. Once the tap or bug goes on, the recording machine starts to operate, and *everything* is taken down, often for weeks and months." The A.C.L.U. also called attention to "the tendency of the courts to rubber-stamp police determinations of probable cause" and give permission for search warrants without looking into the case at hand—a tendency that several other witnesses called "notorious." According to the A.C.L.U., the number of people who would sooner or later be subjected to "this odious practice" was unbounded, for almost everyone has some contact with a criminal or a crime, frequently without knowing it.

By the time the hearings ended, on July 12th, men like Senator Hart were watching the situation develop with growing alarm. "What must be avoided at all costs is a basic confrontation between the legislature and the courts," he said. Chief Justice Warren, in a speech delivered before the chief judges of the fifty federal courts some time later, alluded to the consequences of such a confrontation when he said that "the greatest adhesive power we have is the profound belief of the American people in our constitutional system, the dedication of our public servants to obey its injunctions, and the independence of our judiciary." That power is of necessity compounded mostly of belief and dedication, for the courts have no other means of enforcing their decisions. If that belief were to disappear, to be replaced by a public demand that police power be elevated over judicial power, and if the leading public servants were to set aside their dedication in order to satisfy the people, our form of government would soon end.

Ordinarily, the conservative coalition that dominates Congress exercises negative control, and merely votes down bills, or parts of bills, that it dislikes. In the case of crime control, however, it saw an opportunity to exercise positive control, both in the Senate and in the House of Representatives. During the spring of 1967, Subcommittee

No. 5 of the House Judiciary Committee held its own hearings—in a far more detached manner than McClellan's subcommittee—on the Administration's bill to provide federal funds for research and improvement of local law-enforcement facilities; it then voted to recommend the measure virtually unchanged, and sent it to the full Judiciary Committee, which also approved it and passed it on to the floor. There, in the course of a three-day debate, ending on August 8th, the entire bill was rewritten. According to *Congressional Quarterly*, one of the most widely respected journals in the capital, the result "bore little resemblance to the bill President Johnson had proposed." To begin with, the House version added twenty-five million dollars to the fifty million originally requested by the President, and earmarked the addition exclusively for use in controlling riots and organized crime. In the Administration view, money vitally needed for research, training, and modernizing correctional systems would be used for tear gas and wiretapping equipment instead. Another amendment required that all federal grants provided for in the bill be given to the states to administer, rather than directly to specific localities, as they always had been in the past. This block-grant provision threatened to create a precedent that might ultimately destroy the federal government's right to determine how its money was to be spent. The venerable chairman of the House Judiciary Committee, Emanuel Celler, of New York, who was manager of the bill, took the floor to plead with his colleagues not to transfer control to the states, which, he said, had "no expertise," "no personnel," and "no knowledge whatsoever with reference to coping with these tremendous problems." He got nowhere, and the House passed the revised bill by a vote of three hundred and seventy-seven to twenty-three.

Off and on during September and October of 1967, McClellan called the Senate Subcommittee on Criminal Laws and Procedures into executive session to prepare—or "mark up," as it is called—his own anti-crime bill. The legislative colloquialism was appropriate, for when the bill emerged, on October 30th, it had been marked up beyond recognition. It was widely called a "Christmas-tree bill" —with something hanging from it for just about everyone. At the start of the subcommittee's deliberations, the White House had assured Senators Hart and Kennedy that McClellan had given his promise that he would stop Ervin from adding indiscriminately to the bill. But McClellan did nothing when, time after time, Ervin put a hand into his pocket, saying, "I got a little amendment here," and offered it. Since some of his amendments had scarcely been discussed during the hearings, and one or two of them not at all, Hart and Kennedy tried to delay the vote on them in the hope that the passage of time and the weight of their objections would bring the opposition around to the point where it would consider a compromise they all could live with. Each time, though, Eastland, who rarely attended subcommittee meetings but was on hand for all the critical ones during the marking-up period, would remove a panatela from the center of his mouth and call out, "Vote! Vote!" The votes clicked off, usually five to three in favor, but sometimes six to two, when Scott swung over to the right wing.

The final measure, still known as S. 917, consisted of three principal sections, or, as they later came to be called, titles. Title I was the subcommittee's revision of the House's revision of the Administration's original proposal. The major change in it was that the subcommittee added ten million dollars to the twenty-five million provided by the House for controlling riots and organized crime. If implications of race prejudice were not unmistakable by this time, the bill also provided that Title VI of the 1964 Civil Rights Act, which empowered the federal government to refuse funds to any state or local agency that practiced discrimination, would not apply to funds authorized by this measure. Then, to further insure that the "intent of Congress" was carried out, the subcommittee removed control of the grant program from the office of the Attorney General, whose current occupant was not to the liking of the subcommittee's majority, and placed the operation under a three-man bipartisan board.

Title II constituted the most sweeping attack on the Supreme Court since Franklin Roosevelt tried to expand its membership in 1937. (Francis Allen, dean of the University of Michigan Law School, has concluded that the new assault "may be a more insidious threat, for it is less forthright and candid, and its dangers less apparent to the public at large.") First, this part of the bill included McClellan's proposals overturning the Miranda and Mallory decisions. Second, it included Ervin's amendments limiting the jurisdiction of the Court. Third, it added a new Ervin amendment, to prohibit the Supreme Court and lower federal courts from reviewing any state criminal conviction on a writ of habeas corpus. Often called the "great writ," this dates back to the thirteenth century, and gives any prisoner the right to demand that his jailer justify his detention under the law, and imposes upon the jailer the obligation to do so in open court. Although Ervin's amendment had no effect on the use of habeas-corpus writs within a state's judicial system, it prohibited the federal judiciary from granting them to prisoners who felt that a state had unjustly locked them up. Finally, Title II contained an Ervin amendment to overturn the Supreme Court's decision in United States v. Wade, which had been handed down on June 12th, a month before McClellan adjourned the subcommittee hearings. Although the subcommittee's record was still open then, and left open for several weeks, no specific reference to the Wade case was ever added to it, and so the members had no direct evidence before them on which to base their votes. Nonetheless, they voted six to two in favor of overruling the Court. Briefly, the Wade ruling held that when a suspect was placed in a police lineup before witnesses to a crime, the state had thereby switched from the investigatory to the accusatory stage and that, in keeping with earlier decisions protecting the rights of suspects in criminal actions, identification obtained by such means was inadmissible as evidence unless the defendant had been offered the opportunity to be represented by counsel at the lineup. The ruling was aimed at stopping the police from using tricks like the "reverse lineup" which Chief Justice Warren had commented on in the Miranda decision, and from relying on other common subterfuges, such as putting a short suspect in a lineup of tall men, a young suspect in a lineup of old men, or a black suspect in a lineup of white men. In the Wade opinion, Justice William J. Brennan, Jr., pointed out that eyewitnesses often had little opportunity for a good look at a criminal at the time of the crime, and that at a lineup they were unusually susceptible to suggestion, whether it was intentional or not. Where the witness had also been the victim, he went on, objective identification was even more difficult, because of the unavoidably upsetting nature of such an occasion, often attended by either an open or a covert desire for revenge. Finally, once a suspect had been picked out at a lineup, the witness was almost certain to stick to his identification rather than destroy the state's case by testifying at the trial that he had been wrong or was no longer sure. In any event, Ervin's amendment stipulated that no federal court, including the Supreme Court, could review any determination by a state or federal trial judge that eyewitness testimony was admissible as evidence.

The subcommittee's deliberations on Title II left very

little doubt about McClellan's and Ervin's motives. "They really *hate* the Supreme Court," a participant in the discussions said later. "It's easy for them to use it as a scapegoat to blame all the crime on, because where they come from the Court is already bitterly resented for its civil-rights decisions, and any attack on it is popular. Also, there's no fear in their home states that a bill like this one would destroy our open society, because down there it never has been really open. But both of them know better. They must know that the bill will hurt the poor and yet do nothing about crime. It may be true, to a certain extent, that McClellan actually believes that you can solve the crime problem by locking people up. Of course, that's true, as Hitler and Stalin proved. But even McClellan must know you can't do that without destroying our system. Ervin certainly knows it. He's not only the leading Constitutional lawyer in the Senate—he's smart. All through his career, he's wanted to be named to the Court. Now that it's clear he's never going to make it, he doesn't seem to care what harm he does to those who did make it. He's just plain sore—and a bad loser."

Title III consisted of a revised amendment to control— and permit—tapping and bugging. Around the time of the hearings, the Supreme Court delivered two more opinions on the subject. One, Berger v. New York, reversed the conviction of Ralph Berger, a public-relations consultant to the Playboy Club in New York City, who had been convicted—largely on the basis of evidence obtained through use of a bug—of conspiring to bribe the chairman of the New York State Liquor Authority. The Court held, first, that the state court's authorization to use the bug in this case constituted the sort of general warrant that the Constitution forbids, since the New York law allowed the police, with court permission, to listen in on an alleged criminal without first specifying the nature of the evidence they were after; second, that sixty days, the time the law allowed surveillance of this sort to be carried on, was unconscionably long; third, that the police had not removed the bug after they got the information they wanted; and, finally, that the suspect had not been told before he was tried that his premises had in fact been searched—in the sense that his conversations, like written records, had been taken as evidence. The other case was Katz v. United States, in which the defendant, Charles Katz, had been convicted of violating the federal law that forbade the transmission of betting information via interstate telephone. In this instance, F.B.I. agents had carefully circumscribed their surveillance by placing a bug on the outside wall of a public-telephone booth that Katz customarily used and recording only his side of the conversations that incriminated him. Despite the restraint shown by the agents, the Court ruled that they had violated the Constitution by proceeding without the permission of "a duly authorized magistrate, properly notified of the need for such investigation, specifically informed of the basis on which it was to proceed, and clearly apprised of the precise intrusion it would entail."

Senator Hruska had introduced a new bill, S. 2050, which he claimed included the restrictions laid down by the Court—a claim that was widely disputed by legal scholars. The subcommittee majority combined parts of his bill with parts of McClellan's to produce the final version of Title III. It limited official eavesdropping to periods of thirty days initially, with thirty-day extensions, upon the permission of a federal, state, or local judge in the jurisdiction involved. He was to be apprised beforehand of "the identity of the applicant," "the facts and circumstances relied upon" in the application for a tap or bug, where and how it was to be placed, and "the type of offense or offenses as to which information is to be sought"—none of which seemed to describe the "precise intrusion" to be made, as set down in the Katz decision. In turn, the judge was to determine that a crime had been, was being, or was about to be committed and that police surveillance by way of a tap or bug would produce evidence that could not be found by any other means. The judge was also required to notify the tapped or bugged party that he had been tapped or bugged "within a reasonable time but not later than one year" after the surveillance had ended (unless the judge waived the rule "on good cause"), to keep the tape recordings in question under seal in his court, and to notify a defendant no later than ten days before the recordings were to be used in a trial that they had been made and when (unless the judge decided that there wasn't time and the omission would not be prejudicial). As in the original McClellan bill, Title III gave the President authority to listen in on just about anyone who in his opinion threatened the nation's security. And, in a new provision, Title III permitted "any investigative or law-enforcement officer who determines that . . . an emergency situation exists" to tap or bug whoever was involved for forty-eight hours without so much as going near a judge. Hart and Kennedy contended that this provision, in particular, invited widespread and unrestrained invasions of privacy and opened the door to political intimidation and outright blackmail, but Eastland called out "Vote! Vote!" and the subcommittee's members rejected their argument by six to two. After that, they approved the whole title by the same margin.

Although the two dissenters had known what the outcome of the subcommittee's deliberations would be, they were still appalled by it—since they felt that the bill would allow one corrupt prosecutor and one corrupt judge to harass an entire town or city—and determined to do what they could to block the bill when the full Judiciary Committee met to consider it. Accordingly, they got together with a couple of top officials in the Department of Justice to work out a new strategy. In the end, they decided to introduce what is known as "a clean bill"—that is, one that stands by itself rather than adds to confusion by amending amendments. This one was the Administration's original proposal with a few modifications. At each stage of the drafting process, aides showed the results to McClellan's staff, but when Hart and Kennedy finally offered the clean bill to the subcommittee's parent body, the Judiciary Committee, early in November, McClellan acted thunderstruck and angrily charged that he had been betrayed. In all likelihood, he was hoping to gain a vote or two from uncommitted members who might be inclined to weigh the issue more on the basis of sportsmanship than on its merits. (Another factor that was not lost on anyone who was inclined to join Hart and Kennedy was that while the makeup of the sixteen-member Judiciary Committee was fairly moderate, its leaders—Eastland and McClellan at the head of the majority, and Everett McKinley Dirksen and Hruska at the head of the minority—were conservative allies, and could be relied on to block bills submitted by any members who opposed them.) In any case, McClellan's move failed. Five other Democrats rallied to Hart's and Kennedy's side—Joseph Tydings, of Maryland; Birch Bayh, of Indiana; Quentin Burdick, of North Dakota; Thomas J. Dodd, of Connecticut; and Edward Long, of Missouri—and one Republican, Hiram Fong, of Hawaii, joined them. On the other side were Eastland, McClellan, Ervin, Dirksen, Hruska, Thurmond, and George Smathers, Democrat of Florida. That made it eight to seven in favor of the new measure, with one member being absent— Scott, who had voted for the subcommittee bill but was now in Europe and was expected to stay there until the end of the year. Moving quickly to take advantage of the one-vote margin that Scott's absence provided, Hart pressed for a roll-call vote on the clean bill. Just as quickly, the opposition pointed out that the Senate was in session and if any member objected to a committee session's being held while it was, the rules sustained the objection automatically. Ordinarily, the Judiciary Committee meets only once a week, so that took care of the first week. At the next meeting, Ervin refused to allow a vote because Mc-Clellan, the principal author of the subcommittee bill, was unavoidably detained by his responsibility as chairman of a set of Senate hearings on recent riots. That took up the second week. At the third meeting, McClellan was on hand, but the clean-bill forces feared that he or Ervin would take advantage of the Judiciary Committee's unique "right of holdover"—by which a given topic is automatically held over for a week upon the request of any member, who thereby exhausts the privilege for all members. Fearing that McClellan or Ervin would postpone things merely by talking, without invoking the rule, thus leaving it available for a later meeting, the liberals decided to use it themselves to get it out of the way. That took up the third week. At the following meeting, McClellan's forces, having exhausted their parliamentary delays, threatened to filibuster—a move they could have made at the outset, but at the cost of weariness and frayed tempers all around. That was enough to put off a vote on the clean bill for that meeting, and a few days later, on December 15th, Congress adjourned. Just before it did, Hart and Kennedy warned that unnecessary delays were postponing enactment of *any* anti-crime bill until the following summer, at the earliest, and that in the meantime more thousands of people were being murdered, maimed, robbed, and mugged. A few days before adjournment, the F.B.I.'s quarterly *Uniform Crime Reports* showed that there had been a sixteen-per-cent increase in the crime rate as compared with the first nine months of 1966—the greatest increase since 1958.

When Congress convened again, on January 15, 1968, the Associated Press polled members on what they had found their constituents to be most concerned about during the recess. "Overwhelmingly, the members reported that anger over riots and crime overshadowed all other domestic issues and, in many cases, even the war in Vietnam," it announced. About that time, former Vice-President Richard M. Nixon told the Richmond, Virginia, Chamber of Commerce that the blame for the nation's lawlessness could be laid to the courts, which, he said, "have gone too far in weakening the peace forces against the forces of crime." A few days later, President Johnson delivered his State of the Union Message, in which he said, "There is no more urgent business before this Congress than to pass the Safe Streets Act this year that I proposed last year," and asked that the funds in it be doubled. Three

weeks later, he also sent Congress a special message called
"The Challenge of Crime to Our Society," which contained
a twenty-two-point legislative program. Aside from calling
for passage of the Safe Streets Act, the message proposed
a Juvenile Delinquency Prevention Act, a Right to Privacy
Act, a model crime-prevention project to be added to the
Model Cities Program, the establishment of a strong Corrections Service within the Department of Justice, a comprehensive plan to control drug use, provision of top
priority for the government's so-called anti-racketeer Strike
Forces—a combination of all federal agencies that might
be involved—in cities beset by organized crime, and the
appropriation of funds to hire more policemen, more
F.B.I. agents, and more United States Attorneys around
the country. According to *Congressional Quarterly*, the
message offered "the most comprehensive set of anti-
crime proposals ever sent by a President to Congress."
But according to Gerald Ford, Minority Leader of the
House, "the President has failed to fully recognize the
problem of crime in America and effectively respond to
the challenge." That charge, along with Nixon's, gave
notice that the Republicans had chosen crime as one of
the chief issues in their campaign for the White House. It
did not seem likely that the Supreme Court could escape
playing a role, however passive, in that contest. And if it
didn't succumb to what Justice William O. Douglas has
called the "powerful hydraulic pressure . . . to water down
constitutional guarantees and give the police the upper

hand," it could expect further public demands that Congress take steps to limit its power.

The Senate Judiciary Committee got back to S. 917, as revised by its subcommittee, toward the end of March, 1968. The sections were discussed and acted upon separately, and when Title I, its heavily altered version of the Administration's original bill, came up, Hruska offered an amendment to include the Republican block-grant approach that had been added to the bill in the House version, but lost by one vote. Among the proposals that were adopted were the addition of fifteen million dollars to the grants-in-aid program, bringing the total to a hundred million dollars; an amendment, offered by Edward Kennedy, to set up a National Institute of Law Enforcement and Criminal Justice (similar to the National Institutes of Health), which would provide facilities for research on advanced techniques for police, courts, and correctional systems; and a change in title from the Safe Streets and Crime Control Act to the Omnibus Crime Control and Safe Streets Act—apparently because someone had decided that crime had to be controlled before the streets would be safe. Senator Scott was back in town, and when the showdown vote on the anti-Supreme Court measures in Title II was taken—on a motion to strike out the entire section—he supported McClellan, to produce an eight-to-eight tie. Since a motion fails if the vote on it is a tie, Title II was retained. (For many months, McClellan had been berating the Court for making landmark decisions on narrow margins, like the five-to-four vote in Miranda, but he did not complain about the even narrower margin of his own victory.) Only eleven members of the committee were present when Senator Hart moved to strike Title III, the one dealing with various forms of eavesdropping, and Hart's motion lost by a vote of nine to two, the other affirmative voter being Senator Burdick and the opponents being Eastland, McClellan, Ervin, Bayh, and Tydings on the Democratic side and Dirksen, Hruska, Thurmond, and Fong on the Republican side. On the vote to approve Title III as written, Burdick went over to the majority, making it ten to one, but after the meeting Fong decided that he had miscast his vote originally and recast it with Hart, thus making the score nine to two. Then Burdick did the same, making it eight to three. (Several factors contributed to producing a lopsided vote on Title III. For one, shortly before, Mr. Nixon had announced that he supported wire-tapping as proposed in the bill, which thereupon made it strict Republican policy to support it—a line that was departed from only by Fong. The votes of the conservative Democrats on the committee needed no explanation. Personal considerations were involved in the fact that two of the majority votes were cast by normally liberal members, Bayh and Tydings. The former was up for re-election, and Indiana, his home state, was relatively conservative on most issues but deeply conservative on this one; even so, he straddled the fence by voting for the bill in committee and then announcing in a separate view in the committee report that he had done so reluctantly. But Tydings was not at all reluctant to give his support to the official eavesdropping sanctioned by the bill—in large measure, it would appear, because he had been a United States Attorney before coming to the Senate, and shared the ordinary prosecutor's zeal for any new method that could be used to get at criminals. If the five absentees had been present, the tally would have stood at ten to six.)

At the end of its deliberations, the committee took up a proposal made by Senator Dodd that it add another title to the bill by including a measure of his that had been kicked around on the Hill for nearly five years—a bill to regulate the sale, distribution, and importation of firearms. Dodd appealed for a strong bill, and lost by a vote of eight to five, on the afternoon of April 4th. Less than an hour later, Dr. Martin Luther King, Jr., was assassinated, and then riots burst out in cities around the country, including a particularly violent one in the capital. On April 6th, the committee reconsidered Dodd's proposal, and this time approved it, though not in the form he wanted, by a vote of nine to seven. The amendment, designated Title IV, was exceedingly modest; it exempted rifles and shotguns from all controls, and merely prohibited the sale of pistols and revolvers by interstate mail order to any individual who was not a dealer, along with the sale of handguns over the counter to anyone who was not a resident of the state where the sale was to take place, or who was under the age of twenty-one. Weak as the bill was, it was by far the strongest gun-control measure Congress had ever given serious consideration to.

Senate debate on S. 917 got under way on May 1st—now officially called Law Day, to take the old Socialist May Day taint from it—and when McClellan rose to introduce the bill he took advantage of the occasion to say, "Let us hope that this happy coincidence will overwhelm us as we embark on our deliberations." Before it was all over, three weeks later, the Senate had certainly been overwhelmed by something. When McClellan reached the main point in his opening statement—that the Supreme Court was out to "protect and liberate guilty and confirmed criminals to pursue and repeat their nefarious crimes"—Ervin got to his feet and said, "I ask the Senator from Arkansas if he does not agree with the Senator from North Carolina that members of the Senate who believe that self-confessed murderers, rapists, robbers, arsonists, burglars, and thieves ought to go unwhipped of justice ought to oppose this bill?" The Senator from Arkansas replied, "If I were in sympathy with the criminals, I would vote against the bill," and went on to warn his colleagues that they had "to stand up and be counted on the question: Do you favor turning the guilty loose, or are you going to stand for law and order and protect womanhood and decent citizenship in America and truly make our streets safe?" Bombast may be the rule in Senate debates, but not bombast of this sort, for members do not take kindly to outright bullying. In this case, however, the chamber was, as usual, almost empty, and the two men may have simply meant to enter material in the *Congressional Record* that they could later extract and send home for the edification of their constituents. However, Senator John Sherman Cooper, Republican of Kentucky and the most courtly man in the Senate, had made a special point of being on hand during the exchange because, he explained later, he was appalled by what he had heard about S. 917 and wanted to learn more about it. Finally, after Ervin and McClellan made several more statements about the motives and patriotism of anyone who might disagree with their views, Senator Cooper rose behind his desk and remarked, in a mild voice, "May I say . . . that some of us who expect to vote against Title II do not consider we will be voting against it in the context in which the Senator from North Carolina and the Senator from Arkansas place those who vote thus."

McClellan's most eminent supporter turned out to be Richard Nixon, who had just issued his first position paper on crime. Entitled "Toward Freedom from Fear," the paper accused the Supreme Court of "seriously hamstringing the peace forces" in favor of criminals and called for new laws to "redress the balance" and, if the Court knocked them down, for a Constitutional amendment to the same end. The proper response to crime, according to Mr. Nixon, lay not in cleaning up the slums, where it was bred, but in locking up more malefactors. "If the conviction rate were doubled in this country," he explained, "it would do more to eliminate crime in the future than a quadrupling of the funds for any governmental war on poverty." McClellan also placed in the record an endorsement of S. 917 by the National District Attorneys Association, along with similar endorsements by other groups and individuals—for the most part, the same ones he had included in the hearings record. Finally, he introduced dozens of letters from ordinary citizens around the country praising his efforts. One that he singled out for special mention came from a doctor in Norwalk, Ohio, who wrote, "In many of its recent decisions the United States Supreme Court has caused America and humanity irreparable damages," and enumerated, under headings, subheadings, and sub-subheadings, a score of them, including the damage caused when the Court "abrogated the powers of God," when it added "to the mental illness and emotional instability of the criminal," and when it "laid the foundation—very solidly—for the destruction of this— the greatest country God gave the world—ever!" Senator Stephen M. Young, an elderly Democrat from Ohio, who has been known to deal with crank mail by informing the correspondent that "some crackpot has been writing me letters under your name," took the floor and said that he knew the doctor, and added, "It seems to me astonishing and an indication of weakness that anyone would rest his case in part on a five-page letter from this man who is regarded as a nut." Grim-faced amid general laughter, McClellan stood firm and defended the doctor and his letter by reading more from it, which produced more laughter.

At times, the support of various colleagues also produced more embarrassment than help, as, for instance, when Ervin rose and contended that the majority of the Court's members "wedded themselves to the strange theory that no man should be allowed to confess his guilt, even though the Bible says, even though psychiatrists assert, and even though those interested in the rehabilitation of prisoners declare that an honest confession is good for the soul." Far and away the least helpful ally was Senator Russell Long, of Louisiana, the Majority Whip, who had once been a liberal demagogue and was now merely a demagogue. The American Bar Association had expressed the strongest opposition to the attacks on Supreme Court decisions contained in Title II—an action that McClellan preferred to ignore as much as possible but that Long now brought up. He had been deeply puzzled by the Bar Association's stand, he told the Senate, until he realized that its members "have a vested interest in crime and naturally they would be in favor of striking Title II, because they are in favor of crime." Driving his point home, he added, "They make money out of that." Long also said he had been equally puzzled by opposition from other quarters, and had finally concluded that "it might be a Communist plot to destroy America." Going on to say that "penitentiaries are being emptied these days because of this foolish [Miranda] rule," he warned that things would be far worse in "the new society" if the bill's opponents had their way, because "liberal thinkers would have [made] it absolutely impossible to convict a murderer, arsonist, rapist, or assassin," and "in fact, it would be utterly impossible to convict anyone."

Senator Edward Kennedy had been scheduled to lead a good part of the effort on the floor to strike, or at least weaken, Titles II and III and to strengthen the gun-control provisions of Title IV, but when Senator Robert Kennedy announced that he was a candidate for the Presidency the younger Kennedy told Hart and the others who hoped to bring about fundamental changes in S. 917 that he would be obliged to spend most of his time in the campaign. However, he periodically returned to Washington for important votes, the first of them being one on Title IV, which McClellan, as floor manager of the bill, brought up on May 16th, after two weeks of disconnected and largely unattended debate on all parts of the "omnibus" bill. (McClellan's strategy here was to hold Title I, which the Administration was most interested in getting through, as a hostage to the end, so that the executive branch would not lobby too vigorously against Titles II and III; if it left him pretty much alone, McClellan had promised the Administration earlier, he would not support the block-grant approach added to the bill in the House, which Hruska and his Southern colleagues still hoped to add to the Senate's version.) The key vote was on an amendment that Kennedy had submitted to add rifles and shotguns to the regulations proposed for the sale of revolvers and pistols. No more than a few residents of outlying and lightly populated areas could possibly be put to any hardship if the law was expanded to include long guns, Kennedy told the Senate. "I think that handful of people would be willing to make a slight extra effort in purchasing their firearms in order that two hundred million Americans can sleep and walk and work and play with greater peace of mind," he continued. "That is the question before us, and the results of the way we answer today will be measured in lives saved, robberies avoided, injuries prevented, and snipers disarmed. If we are really serious about doing something about crime and riots and violence, here is our chance." The Senate, under heavy pressure from legions of sportsmen who had been provided by the National Rifle Association and various gun magazines with everything but the facts, turned down the chance by a vote of fifty-three to twenty-nine. (After the assassination of Robert Kennedy, the Senate passed the same bill by a vote of seventy to seventeen.)

Those senators who hoped to defeat Title II and its implicit threat to the Constitution looked to Senator Hart, who had begun to emerge as a leader of the liberal forces in the Senate, to lead them in the campaign against that part of the bill. However, Hart had spent most of the late winter and the early spring leading them in a campaign to enact an open-housing measure, and after eight weeks of constant infighting on the floor—which resulted in a one-vote victory on a motion to impose cloture on a Southern filibuster and, finally, passage of the measure—Hart was exhausted and asked to be excused. In the end, the job fell to Senator Tydings, who, though less skilled than Hart in parliamentary maneuvering, was equally determined to block passage of Title II. "Proponents of Title II urge that it should be enacted to assist in the battle against crime," he said at the start of his presentation to the Senate. "I challenge the assertion. Title II is an attack on the federal judiciary and is not a law-enforcement measure." Although the bill's defenders contended that it would clarify the duties and rights of policemen, prosecutors, and judges, he went on, actually it would create hopeless confusion for them, since they would have to decide, by way of endless discussion and fresh litigation, whether they would abide by the Constitution as interpreted in such cases as Miranda and Mallory or would set out on their own. If they set out on their own, they would have to establish new standards to test the voluntary or involuntary nature of confessions. Tydings illustrated this by saying, "In each jurisdiction, and in each case, the police must in the first instance address such questions as: 'Shall we bring the accused promptly before a magistrate, or shall we continue the interrogation?' 'How long may we continue?' 'How much should we tell a suspect about the charge we are considering?' 'Should we warn him of his right to remain silent?' 'Should we tell him of the consequences of any statement?' 'Should we tell him of his right to counsel?' 'Should we honor his request if he asks for counsel?' 'Should we delay questioning until counsel arrives?' 'Will answers we get without one or more of the above warnings be worth anything in court, or on appeal, or after some future test of Title II's Constitutionality?' " He added, "Each prosecutor must ask similar questions before proceeding. . . . Each trial judge must decide anew—balancing Title II, Mallory, Miranda, and his conscience—whether to admit or deny evidence, or to acquit or convict a person prosecuted with questionable evidence. Each appellate court, perhaps without the benefit of Supreme Court resolution of such issues, must struggle anew with questions now nearly settled prior to the introduction of Title II." As for McClellan's favorite charge that the courts had released the guilty to prey on the innocent, Tydings told his colleagues that the effect of a case like Miranda in this regard would be paltry compared to the effect of Title II. "Ultimately, vast numbers of arrests and convictions made in reliance on Title II would be invalidated by the courts," he argued. "At this point, retrials will in many cases be impossible; witnesses will have died, memories faded. Convicted criminals will be turned out on the streets, and it will be the Senate, not the courts, who will be responsible."

Tydings also addressed himself at length to the contention, made repeatedly by McClellan and his followers, that the number of confessions given to police had fallen off precipitously after Miranda, and that the result had been that the work of law-enforcement agencies had been hampered and countless criminals had been freed. "It is an argument which is popular and appealing, but it is not factual," he said, and went on to cite three studies that had not been available to the subcommittee when McClellan bore down on this subject during the hearings. The first was made at the Yale Law School. Over a period of three months after the Miranda decision was handed down, members of the school's law review sat in on every police interrogation of a criminal suspect in New Haven and, all together, followed a hundred and eighteen cases from interrogation through trial. In eighty-seven per cent of them, they found, the question of confession was irrelevant, since in these cases suspects' statements were not used in evidence. They also found that some of the New Haven police failed to give the warnings required by the Miranda rule and although one-third of the suspects who were not warned made statements, an even larger proportion—fully one-half—of those who *were* warned also made statements. The second study was conducted by the faculty of the University of Pittsburgh Law School, who relied on police and court records rather than on observing the questioning process. These records showed that the number of confessions in the Pittsburgh area had indeed fallen off after the Miranda decision was handed down—by seventeen per cent—compared with a similar period before the decision. But the investigators also found that during the study the conviction rate had remained constant, and that there was still sufficient evidence to hold all but one of the seventy-four suspects who refused to make statements after being arrested. Most important of all, the Pittsburgh study revealed that the rate of "crime clearance" —that is, the number of cases disposed of, with or without a trial, compared with the number of crimes committed— was the same after the Miranda decision as before. The third study Tydings described to the Senate, one conducted at the Georgetown University Law Center, in the capital, over a period of a year, reported that the rate of statements given before and after Miranda in some fifteen thousand cases was the same. Finally, Tydings added, the F.B.I., military courts of justice, and most federal agencies had been using warnings like the one laid down in Miranda for many years and still had maintained far higher rates of conviction than other law-enforcement divisions.

Since McClellan hadn't invited any Constitutional experts or professors of law to give their views of Title II during the hearings, Tydings made up for the omission by soliciting some by letter. Ultimately, he heard from two hundred and twelve legal scholars, including twenty-four deans, at forty-three law schools; all of them condemned Title II. "The effort to legislatively overrule Miranda is unfortunate and illegal," wrote Joseph O'Meara, dean of the Notre Dame Law School. "Unfortunate because Miranda, when all is said and done, does no more than extend to the poor and stupid what the wealthy and sophisticated have had all along. Illegal because it attempts to amend the Constitution by statute, which is a legislative version of what Senator McClellan accuses the Court of." Archibald Cox, a professor at the Harvard Law School and former Solicitor General of the United States, wrote that it was "an exceedingly dangerous precedent for the legislative branch to overturn Constitutional decisions of the Supreme Court," and added, "We live in times in which it is increasingly difficult, yet increasingly important, to maintain the rule of law. I suggest that it would encourage disrespect for law for the Congress to use political power to shut off access to normal judicial process as a method of preventing the enforcement of the Constitution." And the writers uniformly agreed with Hardy C. Dillard, dean of the University of Virginia School of Law, when he stated that "at this juncture in our national life, the last thing we need is to generate an added sense of instability by stimulating a dispute between the Congress and the Supreme Court." The Judicial Conference—headed by the Chief Justice of the United States and composed of all the chief judges of the federal courts—declared its opposition to Title II. The American Bar Association had already taken the same stand, and now its largest local subsidiary, the Bar Association of the City of New York, did, too, saying, "We most strongly urge that the Senate reject Title II."

The opposition to Title II was as bipartisan as the support for it. On May 21st, the day that it was scheduled to be voted on, Senator Edward W. Brooke, Republican of Massachusetts, rose to speak against it. As a former state attorney general, he was probably as familiar as anyone in the Senate with law-enforcement methods, and, as a Negro, he was probably more familiar than anyone else in the Senate with how those methods could be used against the underprivileged. First, he asked whether his fellow-senators were ready to "succumb to a panic which threatens to disrupt our deliberations, which strikes out not at crime but at the courts, which honors 'order' but condemns the Constitution—and which, despite all the claims to the contrary, can have no appreciable effect upon the problem of crime in these United States?" He went on, "The proponents of Title II of this bill would like to persuade us that their argument is with a handful of men who presently sit on the Supreme Court. In actual fact, Mr. President, their argument is with the doctrine of separation of powers, with the federal system, and with our entire structure of government." Across the aisle, Lee Metcalf, Democrat of Montana, who had been a judge on that state's supreme court, took the floor to remind his colleagues that the Constitution was the final law of the land and that the Supreme Court was the final arbiter of what that law meant. "When the Supreme Court misjudges legislative intent, misconstrues legislative language, or points out that a statute is indefinite or obscure, then we, as legislators, have the duty and obligation to examine the decision and correct the wrong legislative interpretation, redefine the crime, or clarify the language," he said. "But Title II of S. 917 does not confront us with either questions of statutory interpretation or a determination of legislative intent. What is at stake here is the inherent right of the Supreme Court to review cases which on their facts present Constitutional questions." One of the effects of such a law, he added, would be a compound fracture of authority, for each of the fifty jurisdictions—the states—would then be able to interpret the Constitution as they pleased. Back on the Republican side, Senator Fong got up to say that a law of this kind would "set an extremely bad precedent" and would encourage Congress to enact "similar legislation whenever the Court handed down a decision with which Congress disagreed."

One point on which opponents of the bill agreed was that the Administration's lobbyists had accomplished far less than had been hoped for. Their principal efforts, it became clear, were aimed at getting rid of the block grants in Title I (which they did not accomplish), keeping that title under the Justice Department's control (which they accomplished, by persuading the Senate to put the three-man board under the Attorney General), providing federal money to supplement the salaries of local policemen (which they accomplished, over the bitter objections of the Southerners, who feared that this form of federal largesse would be used to push integration in police departments), and retaining in the bill permission to use part of its funds for police-community relations—that is, in efforts to lessen friction between local police and ghetto residents (which they accomplished, again over the Southerners' opposition). They also made some attempts to cut out the worst parts of Titles II and III, but, according to a veteran aide of one senator who had the same aim, without much success. "We kept trying to get a decent bill, and Mike Manatos, the White House liaison man on the Hill, kept screaming that they didn't care what kind of a bill they got, just so it was called a crime bill," he said. "McClellan kept telling everybody that the President was not against Title III, and others kept saying that he would accept Title II if the worst parts of it were thrown out. The White House kept denying both statements, but, in any event, the President was less than helpful. He attacked Congress about its failure to enact a stronger gun bill, but he said very tepid things about Titles II and III. The cat was out of the bag then that he wouldn't veto the bill. That was very destructive to our efforts. There was none of that Presidential muscle that could have made it a real race—either through appeals to the people or some phone calls to key senators. As far as I heard, he didn't make a single call over here. And when the bill came to a vote, I never saw anyone from the White House. I guess after the President withdrew from politics everybody else over there did, too."

One of the efforts made by the Administration was to estimate the final vote on a motion to strike Title II, which, it told the opponents of that section, was going to be very close. On the basis of this head count, James Flug, legislative assistant to Edward Kennedy, got in touch with his boss, who was in Oregon campaigning for his brother, and urged him to return for the vote. The Senator did, and shortly before the roll was called he rose on the floor to explain his vote. "Mr. President, each member of Congress recites an oath upon taking office," he said as he stood behind his desk at the rear of the chamber. "He swears to support and defend the Constitution of the United States. Today, each of us has the chance to impart substance to that oath. In essence, we are asked today to determine whether basic Constitutional precepts which lie at the heart of our freedom and our democracy shall be preserved or dissolved. We are asked to decide whether that yellowed document in the Archives, that treaty between ourselves and our forefathers, is to be adhered to or renounced. We are asked whether we have found some substitute for due process of the law, for the assistance of counsel, for the accusatory rather than the inquisitory system of justice, for the great writ of habeas corpus, and, finally, for the Supreme Court as final arbiter of law and guarantor of justice. For it is these keystones in our tradition of ordered liberty which are threatened here today. They are not threatened because they are obsolete, anachronistic, unworkable, unjustified, or unneeded. They are threatened because some Americans have panicked about crime and want scapegoats to flay and panaceas to grasp at. They are threatened because other Americans want revenge against a Constitution and a Court which denounced prejudice and discrimination in large segments of American life. They are threatened because this is a Presidential year, and it is so easy to play politics with questions of law and order. It is ironic that those who rail the loudest about obedience to law as an unshakable absolute, those who inveigh against civil disobedience in all its forms should be in the forefront of an effort to violate the Constitution and rob the Supreme Court of its power. . . . How can the poor feel they have a stake in a system which says that the rich may have due process but the poor may not? How can the uneducated have faith in a system which says that it will take advantage of them in every possible way? How can people have hope when we tell them that they have no federal recourse if they run afoul of the state justice system?"

The motion to strike Title II was defeated not long afterward by a vote of fifty-one to thirty-one—a result that astonished even the title's most optimistic supporters, not to mention the Administration's head-counters. Some of those who voted against the bill ascribed their defeat to the opposition's fear of antagonizing the electorate. A member of the minority later described how he and several other senators had pleaded with a liberal colleague, who was up for re-election, Abraham Ribicoff, Democrat of Connecticut, to join them, only to be turned down with the explanation "Confessions are good. We need confessions." Others saw deeper reasons. One Senate observer, who had been on the floor, in the cloakroom, and along the corridors during much of the debate, put the vote down to what he called "the unsubtle air of racism that prevailed throughout it." Senator Hart got up to say, "Tomorrow's headlines will report our action in a certain fashion. Historians will view it, I think, in an entirely different light. . . . When they get around to writing history, rather than just tomorrow's reassurance to America that we are going to be tough on crime, it will become clear that the Senate made a tragic mistake today. History will tend to interpret today's Senate action in the form of a question: 'Can America afford to extend the protection of the Bill of Rights to all Americans?' "

The next step was to break Title II down into its various parts for a separate vote on each one. McClellan suggested that the debate be limited to twenty minutes per part, with ten minutes for each side. Dirksen broke in and said, "I see no reason why we could not vote right now," whereupon McClellan proposed two minutes to a side. Tydings protested that ten minutes was needed just to inform the members what they were voting on, and Hart said, "Ten minutes is not too long to discuss what we will do with the writ of habeas corpus." Apparently impressed by that argument, Dirksen offered him five minutes. Hart refused, saying, "It just struck me that if anybody does dig back into this *Record* and sees that we allowed ourselves only five minutes apiece to decide what we wanted to do with what the Court has told us the writ of habeas corpus is supposed to mean, it would look a little hasty." With that, Dirksen smiled and, "yielding to the gentle persuasion of my friend from Michigan," agreed to ten minutes to a side.

A motion to strike the section reversing Miranda lost by a vote of fifty-five to twenty-nine; a motion to strike the section reversing Mallory lost by fifty-eight to twenty-six; and a motion to strike the section reversing Wade lost by sixty-three to twenty-one. After the initial vote on Title II, these margins were less shocking to those who had expected a close vote, but the lack of support for the Court led some of them to wonder if the members of the Senate realized what they had been voting on. One aide said he believed that at least half the senators were confused on important points, and explained, "When the roll-call bell rings and a senator goes down to the chamber, he often stops a staff man who's familiar with what's being voted on and gets filled in on it. If he doesn't get a satisfactory answer in sixty seconds, he's likely to walk away and maybe vote willy-nilly." The senator this staff man worked for agreed with this unsettling description of the legislative process, except that in this particular case he put the fraction of his colleagues who didn't understand what they were voting on at three-fifths. But other senators who expressed an opinion on the subject felt that the votes were cast in full awareness of the meaning of the legislation. "The senators were wrong and knew it," Senator Hart said, and he cited the succeeding votes on the Ervin amendments that were most flagrantly un-Constitutional. The one to eliminate Supreme Court jurisdiction over confessions in federal trials lost by a vote of fifty-two to thirty-two; the one to accomplish the same purpose in state trials lost by fifty-one to thirty; and the one to abolish writs of habeas corpus to federal courts lost by fifty-four to twenty-seven; even the section reversing Mallory, which had been retained, was limited by a stipulation that a suspect could not be questioned more than six hours between the time he was taken into custody and the time he was arraigned. Much of the imbalance in the votes won by McClellan and his supporters was laid to the Administration's failure to line up its followers. It was one thing for the Majority Whip to go down the line for the McClellan bill, for even Russell Long cannot depend on Russell Long, but it was quite another for Majority Leader Mike Mansfield to go down the line with the conservative coalition. Some observers and participants ascribed Mansfield's behavior to the Administration's failure to enlist his, or anyone else's, support against even the worst parts of the bill, while others felt that he simply had no idea of the issues at stake. One holder of the latter view said that Mansfield had turned to him during the debate and remarked, "I'm glad I'm not a lawyer and don't have to worry about all these legal points," and then proceeded to enact a law.

"I can only say of this proposed legislation, Mr. President, that it leaves me aghast," Senator Morse said as the debate on the eavesdropping provisions of Title III began. "It is the open and clear invitation to virtually universal bugging and electronic spying upon the American people by federal, state, and municipal police." And Senator Ralph Yarborough, Democrat of Texas, got up and begged his colleagues to reject the invitation. "The Senate has opened a Pandora's box of inquisitorial power such as we have never seen in the history of this country," he said, his voice shaking with emotion. "I think this is the worst bill I have ever seen since I have been a member of the Senate." Across the aisle, Senator Cooper took the floor to point out that the Bill of Rights had been devised specifically to protect the individual against his government, and added, "Now we are setting up, for the first time in this country, an instrument of surveillance which can be misused to reach every individual." Another Republican, Senator Fong, joined in, charging that the bill should have properly been called not the Right of Privacy Act but the End of Privacy Act, for if it passed "it would not be long before the authoritarianism of police rule would be substituted for the authority of law and the majesty of due process." Senator Edward Long, of Missouri, who had spent the better part of three years investigating official abuses of such surveillance and two more years conducting hearings on what he had found, reminded his colleagues of a potential misuse that many of them already knew about but preferred to ignore. "In every metropolitan police department, in almost all of the larger state police departments, and in an alarming number of federal law-enforcement agencies, there is a small cadre of men designated the 'criminal intelligence' activity," he said. "This activity has no specific responsibility for any single crime which has been or is being committed. Its primary fascination is with crimes that are about to be committed. In the pursuit of this fixation, millions of scraps of information—quite frequently gossip—are swept up, evaluated, and stored for some future use. Theoretically, all of this information should tend to furnish some patterns of active criminality. In fact, this activity picks up a lot of embarrassing information on almost everybody in town." Long went on to say that the bill provided the police with a pretext for listening in on anyone who was remotely connected with somebody who was remotely connected with a criminal or a crime, which included just about everyone. And, as an example of the sloppiness with which the law had been drafted, he singled out its definition of the kind of "serious crime" that had to be involved before a tap or a bug could be used—that is, any offense punishable by a year or more in prison. In various states, he continued, penalties of that length were meted out to anyone found guilty of gambling, illicit cohabitation, slander, cruelty to animals, seduction, prizefighting, possessing a gaming device, operating a motor vehicle under the age of sixteen, cutting down trees on someone else's property, or taking someone else's fish.

The real significance of the debate, of course, centered on the value of eavesdropping in law enforcement. "How would it help in the battle against crime in the streets?"

Senator Yarborough demanded. "What purse-snatcher or rapist plans his crime on the telephone?" As for the use of the telephone by criminal syndicates, he pointed out, as others had earlier, that the most immediate effect of the bill would be to cause them to rely on other means of communication. One organized criminal activity covered by Title III was the possession, sale, or use of "dangerous drugs," including marijuana, and this led Yarborough to ask, "Are we going to bug the home of every high-school student to see if we can overhear two teen-agers conspiring to take a puff of marijuana?" That course would be open to law-enforcement officers around the country, he said, and added, "Of course, in the meantime, while [they were] waiting for the teen-agers to say something about marijuana, [they] would overhear and record every intimate detail of family life—every conversation between husband and wife, between father and son, between the father and those with whom he has business." Senator Hart extended the list by adding conversations between client and lawyer, penitent and priest, patient and doctor, and "just innocent people talking to other innocent people." In answer to the claim, made by policemen and prosecutors, that the use of taps and bugs would produce more convictions, Hart retorted, "Rifling the mails and reading private correspondence, suspension of the Fifth Amendment's privilege against self-incrimination, and judicious use of the thumbscrew and rack would probably help the police secure more convictions."

93

In the opinion of many legal scholars, use of Title III would invade not just a person's privacy but also his property, whose sanctity had been guaranteed under Anglo-Saxon law since the fifteenth century. On this point, Fong quoted a famous maxim of William Pitt: "The poorest man may, in his cottage, bid defiance to all the forces of the Crown. It may be frail; its roof may shake; the wind may blow through it; the storm may enter; the rain may enter; but the King of England cannot enter—all his force dares not cross the threshold of the ruined tenement." Hart reminded his colleagues that one of the chief purposes, if not *the* chief purpose, of the Constitution was to safeguard private property. "Make no mistake about it," he went on. "Eavesdropping and wiretapping are trespasses against the home. They are more serious trespasses than an unlawful search of the premises, because they continue over long periods of time unknown to the householder." Above all, though, Hart and his allies were deeply concerned about the provision in Title III that allowed prosecutors to put a tap on anyone for forty-eight hours without a court order if they decided there was an emergency. "I imagine that if one is a good policeman, everything is an emergency," Hart observed. Since the Senate was clearly in a harsh mood, he suggested a compromise on this point —by defining an emergency as a situation "that involves a threat of immediate danger to life." During a brief discussion on this proposal, Senator Frank J. Lausche, a deeply conservative Democrat from Ohio, got up and said,

"I simply cannot conceive that we are going to give an arresting officer the discretionary power to determine that an emergency exists." Senator Robert C. Byrd, a conservative Democrat from West Virginia, was also troubled by this provision of the bill—and, for that matter, by Title III as a whole. "I think wiretapping is a dirty business," he said. Encouraged by this unexpected support from the right, Hart immediately offered an amendment he had wanted to bring up all along—to strike the forty-eight-hour rule altogether. He lost, but only by forty-four to thirty-seven. To Hart, this demonstrated anew that his fellow-senators did understand what they were voting on. And to others it supported their contention that the Administration had failed them, for if it had so much as flexed its muscles—in front of Mansfield, for one, who again voted with the majority—the forty-eight-hour rule would surely have been dropped. In any event, Yarborough finally persuaded the Senate to close the gaping loophole at least partway by stipulating that the rule could be used only in cases involving national security or organized crime. That comforted some who feared misuse of the forty-eight-hour rule, but not many. It still allowed law-enforcement officers to tap or bug on very tenuous pretexts—if, for example, a suspect had patronized a restaurant, a store, or a business that was in any way connected with a crime syndicate, however distantly. Labor leaders, in particular, had reason to fear that the forty-eight-hour rule, along with the rest of Title III, would be open to abuse. The bill singled out for special attention such federal crimes as any "offer, acceptance, or solicitation to influence operations of employee-benefit plans" and "embezzlement from pension and welfare funds," and labor lawyers pointed out that this language would permit a national Administration that happened to be anti-union to listen in on all of labor's affairs, on the ground that someone in a labor organization was believed to be conspiring with someone in a crime organization to mulct union members.

Edward Long, of Missouri, asked the Senate to approve a resolution that assured all citizens of the right to privacy, and was turned down by a resoundingly one-sided voice vote. After that, he asked that permission for tapping and bugging be restricted to crimes that had been or were being committed, and not also cover, as the bill did, crimes that were "about to be committed," and he argued that "to invade the privacy of any citizen of this country on the speculative basis that a crime is about to be committed is to sanction endless 'fishing expeditions' for incriminating information." Senator Cooper concurred, and pointed out that the bill as written provided an unparalleled licence to snoop, unlike the law governing the issuance of search warrants, which were never granted because a crime was alleged to be in the offing, unless a conspiracy was involved, which was a crime in the first place. The second Long amendment went down by sixty votes to eighteen.

Next, Fong tried to get the Senate to cut the thirty-day surveillance period to seven days, and lost on a lopsided voice vote. "The practical effect of all this is to render official eavesdropping very nearly universal," he warned, and added, "I am fearful that if these wiretapping and eavesdropping practices are allowed to continue on a widespread scale, we will soon become a nation in fear—a police state." To control the police in their efforts to control crime—or, as he feared, sometimes in their efforts to commit it—Fong proposed that Title III be circumscribed in the same way that the forty-eight-hour rule had, by limiting its coverage to cases involving the nation's security or the activities of criminal syndicates. The motion got twenty votes. Then Edward Long made one last gesture by moving that Title III be struck from the bill. This motion got twelve votes. With that, Title III was accepted.

When the Senate got around to Title I, the only major issue left to be resolved was over the Republican-backed block-grant approach taken by the House. Faithful to the word he had given the Administration, McClellan voted against block grants, but that one vote was all the Administration got in exchange for its agreement not to oppose him too vigorously on Titles II and III; in effect, his failure to make any effort at bringing his followers along to support the Administration defeated the attempt to stop block grants as decisively as if he had led the fight for them. After agreeing to Edward Kennedy's provision to set up a National Institute of Law Enforcement and

Criminal Justice and disposing of some technical matters, the Senate approved seven other brief titles, the most significant of which stipulated that anyone who was convicted in a federal, state, or local court of "inciting a riot or civil disorder" or "organizing, promoting, encouraging, or participating in a riot or civil disorder" would be ineligible for employment by the federal government or the District of Columbia for five years. This title was clearly aimed at discouraging federal and District employees who lived in the capital from burning it down, as some of them had tried to do following the assassination of Dr. King. But, according to a high official in the Department of Justice, it also constituted an extremely regrettable precedent, for it made anyone who expressed political dissatisfaction by taking to the streets unemployable in the country's largest single labor market. "Even worse, local governments and private businesses can now safely follow suit," he went on. "That can only mean fewer jobs and ultimately more dissension." Then, on May 23rd, the roll was called for a final vote on the entire hundred-and-thirty-four-page package. By this time, no one was surprised that the bill passed easily, but just about everyone was stunned by the overwhelming margin—seventy-two to four. Again the minority was as bipartisan as the majority, with Hart and Metcalf on the Democratic side and Cooper and Fong on the Republican. After it was all over, Mansfield rose to say, "Mr. President, with a loud and clear voice the Senate has said, 'Let us reverse the growing crime rate, let us give our law-enforcement officers the help and assistance they need.' The cry of 'crime in the streets' is not, by any means, a false alarm; it exists and it is about time the Congress faced the issue squarely. With the passage of this measure, the Senate has responded. I think this entire body may be proud of such an immense achievement."

"It was incredible that we got only four votes," Senator Fong said afterward. Hart agreed that it was incredible, but said that he thought he could understand why some senators felt compelled to vote for the bill, aside from the compelling fear that their constituents would pay them back at the polls if they didn't. "When you're faced with a bill that you think is bad and yet the mood of the country is overwhelmingly for it, then a case can be made for voting in favor of it on the ground that you're doing what the voters want you to do," he said. "Of course, that raises the most serious questions about the meaning of representation. One of them is whether it's just an alibi when we vote as our constituents want us to vote, not as we believe we should vote. But a more difficult question arises when it comes to voting in a way that will make the public feel that their government is against them. Some men in the Senate feel that if it is a real possibility that the people will lose their faith in the government's ability to protect them—in this case, against crime—then the vote must be cast to reassure them that the government is on their side, even if the bill is bad. I don't share that view, but it may be what happened here." To Senator Metcalf, the outcome was bad whatever the reasons for it may have been. "This act is the height of irresponsibility!" he said, slamming a fist into the palm of his hand. "Many of those who voted for it believe that it's un-Constitutional, and it patently is. We have as much responsibility to carry out the intentions of the Constitution as the President or the courts, and we haven't met it—not at all. The Supreme Court will undoubtedly overturn most of the law, but, by the time it does, the right wing may have got the public so stirred up that it will be ready to give the police extraordinary powers without even realizing what it's doing." For his part, Senator Fong put the bill down as "the most vicious piece of legislation that has passed the Senate in my time." And Senator Cooper predicted, "It will return to haunt us." While the four senators put varying emphases on different parts of the bill as their main reason for opposing it, they agreed that even if it was not un-Constitutional they would have voted against it on the ground of policy alone. "The reversal of Miranda, Mallory, and Wade will hurt the poor and do nothing to lessen crime," Hart said. "And legalized eavesdropping will set back the whole society, but especially the affluent, who are more susceptible to blackmail and intimidation."

Three of the dissenters—Metcalf, Cooper, and Fong—said that their votes had not placed them in political jeopardy. "It was not hard for me to vote as I did," Metcalf said. "We don't have big cities in Montana. We don't have

a high crime rate. We don't have many Negroes." (Of
course, Senator Mansfield, who is also from Montana,
went along with the majority.) Of the four dissenters,
Senator Hart was the only one who faced a clear danger
in voting against the bill; Michigan contains a number of
large and middle-sized cities with high crime rates, racial
unrest, and white minority groups that can produce a back-
lash against both Negroes and politicians who stand up
against bigotry. As a result, some of Hart's aides had advised him to support the measure, but at least one of them
counselled him to oppose it, and argued that otherwise he
would later be blamed for misleading his constituents
when the crime rate continued to rise in spite of the new
law. "I never stewed about it," Hart said. "I just decided
it was a bum bill." But he conceded that his stand would
undoubtedly be used against him when he ran again in
1970, and cited the cascade of mail he had received from
constituents attacking him for his position. "They feel
that if you didn't vote for the crime bill, you're just out of
touch and don't know—or, worse, don't care—what's
going on back home," he explained. "In 1970, my opponent will be bound to use this. He'll say something like
'One of the great domestic crises facing this nation is its
crime rate. Only four senators were so insensitive as to
vote against the Omnibus Crime Control and Safe Streets
Act. They forgot the abiding interests of the people in their
overriding concern for the welfare of criminals.' " Having
prepared his opponent's campaign for him, Hart went on

to mention that far graver political retribution was in store for two of the three senators who had not been present for the final vote but had announced that if they had been they would have voted nay—Morse and Ernest Gruening, of Alaska—because they were both up for re-election in 1968, when the voters' memories would be fresh. (The third man to announce that he would have voted against the bill was Young of Ohio, who had been elected to his second term in 1964, at the age of seventy-five.) Not long after the Senate vote on the crime bill, Gruening went down to defeat in a primary election, and although the main issue in it appeared to be his advanced age, it was believed that his stand on the crime bill had not helped him. He ran a write-in campaign, but lost in November. And the final tabulation of votes in Oregon showed, after a recount, that Morse had been beaten by a very narrow margin—probably because of this one vote.

Of the twenty-one other absentees, eleven announced that they were for the bill, and ten took no position. Some of those who took no position were, as the *Record* indicated, "necessarily absent," including the three senators who then or later were active as candidates for the Democratic Presidential nomination—Robert Kennedy, Eugene McCarthy, and George McGovern. Others, including Vice-President Humphrey's campaign managers—Senators Fred R. Harris, of Oklahoma, and Walter F. Mondale, of Minnesota—were in town at the time and unnecessarily absent. One insight into why some of those who did not vote and did not announce how they would have voted if they had could be found in the situation faced by a senator like Frank Church, Democrat of Idaho, who was engaged in a re-election campaign. Faced with the toughest fight of his career, chiefly because of his long-standing opposition to the war in Vietnam, Church had concentrated a large part of his campaign on another issue that he had long been outspoken about—opposition to any form of gun regulation, which has always been anathema to just about everyone in Idaho. It was now about the only thing he had going for him, and he had repeatedly promised his constituents that he would vote against such a bill no matter what happened. A vote for the crime bill might have pleased residents of a city like Boise, where there was enough crime to be noticed, but it would have cost him dearly throughout the rest of the state, because his vote would have helped to pass the gun section, too. And a vote against the bill would undoubtedly have been picked up by his right-wing opponent and touted as an expression of Church's softness on domestic as well as foreign enemies.

Senator Edward Kennedy had planned to be on hand for the roll call, but it came about a day earlier than the leadership had anticipated, and he was in a hotel room in Harrisburg, Pennsylvania, where he had been campaigning for his brother. When the vote came up, Flug, his legislative assistant, telephoned the Senator and inquired how he wanted to be recorded. Despite his concern about the dangers inherent in Titles II and III, Kennedy felt that something might still be done to limit them if the right tactics were used. With this in mind, he asked for his assistant's recommendation, and Flug replied that if he were a senator he would vote against the bill. "And what would you do if you were a senator's legislative assistant?" Kennedy asked. "I would recommend a vote for it or no vote at all," Flug answered. After a pause, the Senator called for the arguments favoring an affirmative vote, and Flug enumerated them: the bill contained Kennedy's amendment providing for an Institute of Law Enforcement and Criminal Justice; Title I, except for the block-grant provision, was a step forward; Title IV, even with its failure to regulate rifles and shotguns, was better than nothing; and the worst parts of Titles II and III could possibly be modified if the Senator was appointed to the House-Senate conference committee to work out the final form of the law. When Flug finished, Kennedy pointed out that he would have a far better chance of being appointed to the conference committee as a supporter of the measure than as an opponent, since he himself had argued during a fight on a congressional redistricting bill that those who vote against a measure should not be allowed to be conferees and thereby carry on their opposition to a measure that the Senate, which they are supposed to represent in conference, has already approved, and the argument was certain to be remembered when Eastland chose members of the Judiciary Committee to take up the crime bill in conference.

Kennedy also pointed out that if the conference did not adequately repair the bill's defects, he would have another chance to vote against it when it was sent back by the conferees for a final vote in the Senate. With that, he instructed Flug to announce that if present he would have voted for the Omnibus Crime Control and Safe Streets Act.

Some senators who lacked such a rationale felt sufficiently unhappy about their vote to admit it. "Several colleagues who voted for it told me privately that they disagreed with the bill and agreed with me," Cooper said. Others shared the view expressed by one member who said, "I just couldn't vote against a bill with a title like that in a year like this." And still others had no explanation for the Senate's action at all, like one senator who merely shook his head and said, "Weren't we terrible there?" For some, it was apparently all right to be terrible as long as other people weren't. Jacob Javits, of New York, who voted for the bill, addressed the graduating class of the law school at the State University in Buffalo a few days later and took the opportunity to warn his audience, "If the citizens are not vigilant to defend the integrity of the Court on Constitutional questions, we run the risk of developing a dictatorship of the majority, which could extinguish individual liberty, all under cover of the 'emergency power' to suppress crime." That outcome, he added, would inevitably create "a confrontation dangerous to the Constitution, a confrontation that could lead to a Court-packing effort or a new effort to take appeals jurisdiction away from the Court entirely."

When the House met, on June 5th, to take up the Omnibus Crime Control and Safe Streets Act, it turned out that a confrontation of the sort Javits described was just what many representatives were looking for. The day before, Representative Paul G. Rogers, Democrat of Florida, had let it be known that the supporters of the bill enacted by the Senate meant to confound the hopes of men like Edward Kennedy by pushing the measure through the House without a conference, to ensure that the anti-Supreme Court provisions remained in it as written. Rogers had obtained permission from the Rules Committee to offer a motion to this effect on the floor, and it was widely expected to pass. Early on the morning of the fifth, Senator Robert Kennedy was shot in Los Angeles, and that crime (which some members publicly blamed directly on the Court's "softness on criminals") made absolutely certain what had been virtually certain before it happened—that the crime bill passed by the Senate would be passed by the House unchanged. "There is an emotion in the House today amounting to a passion that is not going to be frustrated, and is not going to be denied," Charles Mathias, Jr., a Republican congressman from Maryland, told his fellow-members when they met that afternoon to consider the Senate bill. Emanuel Celler, who would have preferred to see the bill defeated altogether rather than passed in its existing form, desperately tried to divert the passion, pleading that the bill be sent to conference for refinement and warning that in any clash between Congress and the Supreme Court "Congress cannot be the winner." Minority Leader Gerald Ford disagreed with Celler. "I refuse to concede, Mr. Speaker, that the elected representatives of the American people cannot be the winner in a confrontation with the U.S. Supreme Court," he declared. "To admit that is to admit that the American people cannot control the U.S. Supreme Court. I think the American people today must have some control and jurisdiction over the judiciary of the federal government." Of course, if they did—and made the Court subject to popular whim—the American form of government would thereby cease to exist.

Robert Kennedy died early on the following day. A few hours later, the Speaker of the House, Representative John McCormack, told a group of reporters in his office that the Kennedy family had requested that Congress carry on with the business of the nation, and he said that the most important part of that business would be the debate and the final vote on the Omnibus Crime Control and Safe Streets Act, which would begin at three o'clock that afternoon. When public clamor over a great issue reaches the stage where it can no longer be ignored, the House of Representatives ordinarily responds by doing the wrong thing—not to resolve the issue but to stop the noise. This time, it did the wrong thing in Robert Kennedy's name. (If it does the right thing, it ordinarily does it at the wrong time. After Dr. King was assassinated with a rifle, Congress passed a law to regulate the sale of pistols, and after Senator Kennedy was assassinated with a pistol, Congress passed a law to regulate the sale of rifles.) More than two hours were devoted to tributes to the fallen Senator, most of which contained pleas that the House unanimously enact the crime bill as revised by the Senate as a memorial to him. (On a C.B.S. television interview the following day, Peter Edelman, the late Senator's legislative assistant, angrily criticized this attempt to cash in on the tragedy, pointing out that the bill "contains measures that Robert Kennedy very deeply opposed"—in particular, Titles II and III.)

The tone of the House "debate" was set by members like Watkins M. Abbitt, Democrat of Virginia, who trotted out the old charge that criminals had been "encouraged, pampered, and nurtured not only by the majority of the Supreme Court and certain segments of the judiciary but by many other leaders in government," and Ray Blanton, Democrat of Tennessee, who served notice that "Congress will no longer abdicate its responsibilities to nine appointed men, nor will it allow the passivity of an appointed Attorney General to be a roadblock in our disgust and anger and our wrath over the permissive society of crime." One surprisingly candid statement in support of the bill came from Representative John G. Dow, a Democrat from upstate New York, who said, "This bill, as now amended,

I regret exceedingly, and will only vote for it because of the widespread desire of all our people to curb crime and prevent continuation of violence in our land. As the price for this, we are saddled with amendments that threaten our liberties and may remain to haunt us. I am voting for this measure out of deference to so many expressions from constituents in my district who regard protection in our streets as their paramount anxiety today." In the end, three hundred and sixty-eight representatives voted to accept the Senate bill, seventeen voted not to, and forty-eight did not vote at all.

Under the Constitution, the President has ten days, excepting Sundays, in which to sign a bill. When a week passed without President Johnson's having affixed his signature to the Omnibus Crime Control and Safe Streets Act, speculation arose that he would either veto it or let it become law without his signature. But in view of his earlier failure to take a public stand against the bill, it seemed unlikely that he would now deprive members of his party of the chance to claim credit for doing something about crime when they went home to face the electorate —a claim that would have been greatly weakened either by his veto, even if it was later overridden, or by his refusal to sign the measure. "What is he waiting for?" Congressman Ford demanded, as if now that the Court had been put in its place it was time to turn to the Presidency. Finally, on June 19th, the last day left for his approval, President

Johnson, saying that the bill "contains more good than bad," signed it—an act that the *Times* described as "a surrender to public hysteria."

Hysteria about crime and about the role attributed to the Court in creating it was rising even more rapidly than crime itself. Late in June, the F.B.I.'s *Uniform Crime Reports* showed that the crime rate was up by seventeen per cent for the first quarter of 1968. Two weeks later, the Gallup Poll organization stated, "Today, unfavorable feelings toward the Court outweigh favorable sentiment by a 3-to-2 ratio"—the first time that a negative response had been recorded. A few weeks after that, a Louis Harris poll showed that the trend was growing apace, for now the ratio was three to one against the Court, and by this time nearly seventy per cent of those polled believed that "violation of law and order has been encouraged by the courts."

It was largely because of this public attitude that the conservative coalition in the Senate, which had helped create it in the first place, was able to block the nomination of Justice Abe Fortas to be Chief Justice—and, in large measure, to deny the Court the independence that the authors of the Constitution had tried to assure it. At the start, the move was not an attempt to undercut the Court, or even to reprimand Fortas for his questionable conduct in office, about which nothing was known at the time. Rather, it was an example of the truism that in politics one man's preferment is paramount to the public safety. On June 21st, Senator Robert P. Griffin—a Republican from

Michigan who had moved up from the House two years before when Governor George Romney appointed him to fill the unexpired term of the late Senator Pat McNamara, and had then won a term on his own—rose to announce, "I shall not vote to confirm an appointment of the next Chief Justice by a lame-duck President." In a Constitutional sense, the statement was absurd, for it suggested that any President at any time during his second term in office lacked Presidential powers. But in a political sense it quickly took on meaning, as McClellan, Ervin, Eastland, and others in their camp saw still another opportunity to weaken, and perhaps even control, the Court. It was reported that Griffin was rather embarrassed by the allies who joined him in what had been for him little more than a partisan gesture but that he was prepared to go along with them, because he now saw a chance to wrest control of the Republican leadership in the Senate from Minority Leader Dirksen, who was having increasing difficulty in keeping the younger members of his party in the Senate in line. Dirksen had dismissed the Griffin move as "frivolous, diaphanous, gossamer" when it was first made, but he soon saw reason not to underestimate the challenger, for Griffin had led the House fight, in 1965, that unseated Minority Leader Charles Halleck in favor of Ford. When it became clear that Fortas's defeat was inevitable, Dirksen took the only step he could to weaken the threat to his own position, and joined the rebellion. In the end, fewer than half the senators voted to invoke cloture to cut off a filibuster by the anti-Fortas coalition led by Griffin, and that ended the effort to confirm the nomination. It also recalled a warning issued by Chief Justice Warren before a conference of federal judges in Philadelphia a few weeks earlier. "If one of our three co-ordinate branches of government is discredited, the entire structure of government is weakened," he said. "None of them can strengthen the democratic process by climbing over the weakened body of another. In the nature of things, the judiciary is the most susceptible to attack, be-cause it cannot enter the political arena and trade blow for blow with those who would discredit its work. The others can and do."

Still, it seems unlikely, even in this time of change, that the Supreme Court will collapse under some future assault manned by a vengeful public and led by a pliant Congress or President. Instead, the worst prospect is that the Court will resolve the issue by retreating from it, either because the current majority will be afraid not to retreat, as the only means of preserving that institution, or because a new majority appointed by a new President will want to. In either case, the Court might well allow the reversal of its recent decisions and the use of secret police surveillance to stand—or at least approve them in substance—and thereby make the police power superior to its own. His-torically, of course, that kind of compromise has often brought on tyranny.

# INDEX

# Index

# Index